To Nora,

Looking forward to a long and successful "journey" in all your "desire" and pursuits

Curiosity
AND THE
Desire for Truth

12/18/15

ADVANCE PRAISE

Dr. Velvl Greene, a wise and deeply humane scientist, tells us in this lively and engaging book about a remarkable spiritual quest following an encounter with one of the greatest spiritual leaders of the 20th century, the Lubavitcher Rebbe, Rabbi Menachem Mendel Schneerson. This is a book that will inspire and amuse at the same time — a wonderful read that will leave you feeling spiritually and intellectually refreshed.

— Rabbi Lord Jonathan Sacks,
Emeritus Chief Rabbi, United Hebrew Congregations of Britain
and the Commonwealth

This is a fascinating story of a unique friendship between the scientist Professor Velvl Greene and Rabbi Menachem M. Schneerson, a student of science, of all Jewish learning, and of course the Lubavitcher Rebbe. You will learn much from this book. It will challenge, reassure, and move you.

— Joseph Telushkin, author,
*Rebbe: The Life and Teachings of Menachem M. Schneerson,
the Most Influential Rabbi in Modern History*

Dr. Velvl Greene's memoir is an uplifting account of some very insightful interactions between a prominent scientist and the late Lubavitcher Rebbe, Rabbi Menachem Mendel Schneerson. Dr. Greene carves a Judaism that is intelligent, authentic, and self-reflective; and through joining the author on his journey, the reader is drawn into the post-apologetic era where faith and science can comfortably cohabit. A delightful and very personal contribution to Torah–science literature.

— Rabbi Chaim Miller, author,
Turning Judaism Outward: A Biography of the Lubavitcher Rebbe; compiler, *Chumash,
The Gutnick Edition*

From its preface to its epilogue, *Curiosity and the Desire for Truth: The Spiritual Journey of a NASA Scientist* is a masterful presentation of divine providence, science, and religion, and a unique philosophical approach to Judaism, including the author's extensive interaction and experiences with the late Lubavitcher Rebbe. We are fortunate to have access to Dr. Greene's invaluable lectures, articles, correspondence, and interviews, all in one volume.

— Fred Rosner, MD, MACP, professor of medicine (emeritus),
Mount Sinai School of Medicine, New York, NY

Thank you for giving me the opportunity to review this wonderful book. I read it through several times and found it engaging, captivating, and entertaining each time. With a simplicity that belies its brilliance, it challenges the reader to follow in Professor Greene's unrelenting quest for truth and for continuing spiritual growth. Those who knew Professor Greene will recognize his own unique voice on every page, with his typical zeal and respect, and his knack for pointing out the humorous ironies of the world — all of which come from his recognition that we are all but a tiny part in this huge wonder called *creation*, yet how fortunate we are to be able to make a profound difference.

— Ben-Tzion Pape, educator, chaplain, and
shaliach (emissary) of the Lubavitcher Rebbe,
Little Rock, AR

These writings of Professor Velvl Greene reflect the career and beliefs of a remarkable man. They tell the story of a scientist who grew in faith and observance, and effortlessly united different worlds in a search for truths that are eternal. I had the pleasure of personally knowing Professor Greene, and this book brought back many memories.

— Michael H. Silber, MB, ChB,
professor of neurology, dean, Mayo School of Health Sciences,
Mayo Clinic College of Medicine

A fascinating and inspiring saga of a scientist's search for meaning in life and of his courageous willingness to act on its discovery. An intimate and gripping glimpse into the soul of a Jew returning joyfully to his roots.

— Shimon (Seymour) M. Glick, MD,
professor (emeritus, active), Faculty of Health Sciences,
Ben-Gurion University of the Negev

A splendid collection of wise and humane reflections on life and truth by a distinguished scientist and Torah-loving emissary of the Lubavitcher Rebbe. Velvl Greene's insights about Judaism and science, and his examples about how each can illuminate the other, are useful correctives to the common (and mistaken) belief that they are incompatible. Tales from his own improbable spiritual journey and his encounters with the Rebbe, and his account of the true miracle of birth, both warm the heart and inspire reverential awe regarding the possible presence of Providence in our lives.

— Leon R. Kass, MD, PhD, professor emeritus,
The Committee on Social Thought, The University of Chicago

CURIOSITY
AND THE
DESIRE FOR TRUTH

The Spiritual Journey of a NASA Scientist

Dr. Velvl Greene

AN ARTHUR KURZWEIL BOOK
New York/Jerusalem

AN ARTHUR KURZWEIL BOOK
11 Bond Street #456
Great Neck, NY 11021

First edition

Letters by the Lubavitcher Rebbe are used with permission from the estate of Rabbi Menachem M. Schneerson and from the Kehot Publication Society.

Cover image of Dr. Velvl Greene: Howard Lower, owner, Lower Photography & Studio.

Back cover photo copyrighted by, and used with permission of, Jewish Educational Media, Inc., The Living Archive. Photograph by Chaim B. Halberstam, November 3, 1991.

Front cover design: Linda V. Curran

Interior and back cover design: Judith M. Tulli

Dr. Velvl Greene
Curiosity and the Desire for Truth
The Spiritual Journey of a NASA Scientist

ISBN: 978-0-9855658-7-9

TABLE OF CONTENTS

PUBLISHER'S NOTE

Dr. Velvl Greene did not have this book in mind when he wrote the contents before you.

The son of Soviet Jewish immigrants, Greene forged a dichotomous path to become both a NASA scientist in the search for life on Mars and a confidante of Rabbi Menachem Mendel Schneerson, the Lubavitcher Rebbe. We are indeed the fortuitous beneficiaries of his writings on these and other diverse and thought-provoking subjects.

Under the careful and dedicated direction of Dr. Greene's two sons, Rabbis David and Shmuel Greene, his recorded lectures and interviews were transcribed and edited, his journal articles and correspondence were gathered and, from this rich material, the present book was sculpted. Working closely with Wendy Bernstein, who brought her superb professional editorial talents and skills to the project, this powerful book emerged. The result is an extraordinary and unique spiritual memoir.

The reader is asked to note the following:

1. The Foreword by Rabbi Adin Steinsaltz is a transcript of remarks made on the occasion of the 30th day after Dr. Velvl Greene's funeral.

2. Rabbi Moshe Feller, who readers will encounter in these pages, is a native and longtime resident of Minneapolis, MN. He began his activities in his hometown as a senior emissary of the Lubavitcher Rebbe in the early 1960s.

3. Rabbi Menachem Mendel Schneerson was known to have

written thousands of letters during his life, including a long, intense, and life-changing correspondence with Dr. Greene. Excerpts from the personal letters exchanged between the Rebbe and Velvl Greene appear throughout this book, and are indicated by a typewriter icon.

— Arthur Kurzweil

Publisher

June 2015

ACKNOWLEDGMENTS

Our father was a multi-faceted man of many interests, as you will discover in this book. It is hard to note the many influences in his life that made him who he was. We would like to think that one of the most valued things in his life was family, and we are certain that the fact that his wife and children worked together with many friends and relatives to put together this book would cause him to beam with pleasure (*nachas*).

We are grateful to our mother, Gail Greene, who joined her life to our father in June 1956, and even now encourages others to know of his gifts and witticisms.

He would never have become who he was without the influence of his grandmother, Rochel Hornick; his parents, Sam and Sarah Greene; and his in-laws, Max and Ann Chesler, who regarded him as their son. He showed his love to people who became his family members, not only the ones he was born to.

We acknowledge with love our family's participation and help in putting this book together, specifically Joe and Ziona (Zed) Bellan, his oldest sister and her husband, who was truly an older brother for our father; Irvine and Geulah (Julie) Margolese, his second sister and her husband, who taught him so much; Dr. Harold and Gerry Kipper, our mother's older sister and her husband; and Dr. David and Sandy Dietz, our mother's youngest sister and her husband. We would be remiss to not mention the in-laws of his children, who truly became family to our father, opening their arms and homes to all of us: Michael and Rebecca (Ruby) Black, Fred and Bernice Seidel, Scholom Ber and Esther Raskin, Dr. Baruch and Rifka Kahana, and Dr. Kenneth and Susan Kunzman.

During his student days, when he first arrived in Minnesota, cousin Max and Minnie Greene were his family and support.

Among those in Minnesota who welcomed him into their homes for Shabbos lunch, after a long trek to their neighborhood *shul*, were Herb and Rose Joshua and Sam and Helen Ziff. Lenny and Charlotte Aizman, who knew he liked his barbecue and beer, became very close friends.

When our parents settled into life in Beersheva, Prof. L'Chaim Naggan and Prof. Shimon Glick and his wife, Brenda, were essential to their feeling at home.

And there are those who started out as his students, lodgers, and guests and became family — like Reuven and Dr. Kim Amrami, Shabtai and Elana Hadjbi-Drori, Shmuel and Chana Sa'ad, and Dr. Sol Jaworoski and his wife, Dr. Eve Finkelstein.

In 1977, during their first sabbatical in Israel, our parents became close friends, neighbors, and admirers of Dr. Elchanan and Shira Leibowitz (now Schmidt), and mourned for Elchanan upon his passing as keenly as if he were a "blood" brother. This type of neighborly relationship was also created with Yehuda and Sima Tamir and Cyril and Golda Simkin.

No words can express our thanks to our father's teachers and learning partners, Rabbi Chaim Mackler and Prof. Mordechai (Macky) Goldman and his wife. They were like long-lost brothers to our father, and heartfelt friends.

Our father's story would be totally incomplete if no mention were made of those who helped him on his spiritual journey in seeking truth. Our father's trek actually began with the vision of our grandparents, who enrolled their children in the Peretz Shul and HaBonim Youth Group, both in Winnipeg. Pioneer Women of

Winnipeg, an absolute part of our grandparents' home, directed our father's Zionist feelings. In later years, he assumed the mantle of president of Herzl Camp, which was dedicated to teaching Zionist ideals to youngsters in the Midwest.

Our father merited to meet Rabbi Moshe and Mindy Feller, Chabad emissaries to Minnesota, in 1962. These people no doubt changed his life and opened his eyes. Through them, he was introduced to the Lubavitcher Rebbe, Rabbi Menachem Mendel Schneerson, who challenged our father, taught him, inspired him, and respected him.

This undertaking would not have happened if not for the help of those who loved our father in return for his love, and graciously have helped finance this book, including Eduardo Elsztain, Yossi Azaraf, Alexandra Amrami, and our cousins, Dr. Fred and Rochel Cooperstock, Lindy (Sharada) Filkow, Dr. Sam and Rona Kipper, and Addie and Alysa Gisser. In addition, our father's first granddaughter, Sara Tikva Black.

— Rochel Naomi, Peninah Miriam, Dovid Isser,
Nechamah Denah, and Shmuel Yaakov
Israel
United States
2015

FOREWORD

Why do people seek the truth?

For some people, the search for truth is like the searches that kittens do. Kittens stick their noses everywhere, they sniff things, turn them upside down, peek into nooks — not for any profound philosophical reason, but because they are endowed with a quality that is neither simple nor self-evident: They are curious.

Curiosity is possibly typical of young age — for kittens, like human beings, do not remain young forever, and as they grow up they lose most of their curiosity.

An interesting experiment was once done: Two babies — a human baby and a baby chimpanzee — were raised together, and given the exact same treatment. At first, the chimpanzee did much better than the human baby — he learned much faster to ride a bicycle, to use a fork and spoon, etc.; but around three years of age his curiosity gradually began to disappear, and from that point on, he remained a monkey, while the human baby continued to develop in all areas.

Perhaps the difference between ordinary people and scientists or artists is that creative artists and men of science remain children, to some extent. There are people who, even if according to an ophthalmologist their eyesight is excellent, see nothing — possibly because there is nothing in the brain behind their optic nerve; while others look at anything and everything with wide open eyes — trees, shrubs, grimaces — and turn it into poetry or science.

People may pass by a sunflower field, and one person will paint it in such a way that people will be willing to pay $15 million for it; others will not see them at all; and others may say, "Oh yes, that's right, sunflowers." Or the proverbial American tourist who, after visiting the Western Wall for the first time in his life, said, "It's a western wall just like all western walls."

A popular science book about modern physics, written by Albert Einstein and another professor, begins as follows: Modern physics starts with electricity. How was electricity discovered? Let us take two people, each of whom has a rod of glass, a piece of silk cloth, a bit of amber, and some flannel. A decent person will probably use the glass rod as a bookmark, with the silk cloth he will clean his eyeglasses, he'll use the amber as a weight on his papers to keep them from flying in the wind, and with the flannel he will polish his shoes. Such a person will never discover electricity.

Who will? A person who has nothing to do, the kind of person who in good Yiddish is called a *leidiker*. Such a person will rub the glass pole with the silk cloth, and then discover that it attracts all sorts of things. Then he will rub the amber with the flannel, and discover that the amber now also draws to itself various things. Then he will notice that the glass and the amber do not attract things to them in the same way, because one has what we now call positive power, and the other has negative power. This was the beginning of all that we know today about electricity, knowledge that is applicable also in molecular biology and many other fields.

Why on earth would anyone want to rub a glass rod? What reason would one have to do so? Yet this is precisely where science begins: in the curiosity of a person who does not really have a good reason to be curious. A person who opens doors in order to look for food or try to find the way out of a labyrinth does not do that out of curiosity. Curiosity is when a person opens doors even though he has no reason to do so.

In one way, human curiosity is not very different from curiosity of kittens. Kittens do not really look for anything specific, and therefore also do not find anything, unless by coincidence. Human beings, too, may find some useful things by coincidence (and still call it *scientific research*), and so it will turn out that curiosity is not entirely useless. Yet the starting point would be curiosity, and the practicality will only be secondary.

For instance, only 1 percent of all of the science of mathematics is applicable in any practical manner, while 99 percent of mathematics has no use whatsoever. Professor Greene's researches, too, did not have too much practical significance; maybe sometime in the future something practical will grow out of it, and perhaps it will always remain in the realm of fantasy literature. A significant portion of what is being done in universities is, in fact, no more than advanced kittenship. There are kittens that one holds in one's hand, and kittens that campuses are built for, but both do basically the same thing: checking out what is happening in this nook or that cranny.

However, there is another level to these searches. When a mathematician is asked, "Why do you care if a certain number is a congruent of such and such number in such and such a modus?" — he'll say, "Because I want to discover the truth!" This desire is very different from the childish desire to know what is going on.

The question, "What is truth?" is a very wide topic. Maimonides, in the beginning of his great book, says that absolute truth is that which is eternally true. Whatever is not eternally true is only relative, temporary truth. Therefore only God is absolute truth, because only God is eternal.

Thus curiosity and the desire to seek for truth are, in fact, the search for God. How do we know that God is somewhere? When He signs His Name, and "God's seal is truth" (Babylonian Talmud, Tractate Shabbat 55a). Wherever there is truth of any kind, there is God's *signature*, His *seal*. The search for the absolute is not the kittenish search: It is the desire to touch, somehow, God's seal, even if that specific thing will not be useful today, tomorrow, or ever.

The search for the absolute, the relationship with the transcendental, with that which is beyond all limits, is part of the human spirit, the breath of life that God "breathed into his [Adam's] nostrils" (Genesis 2:6), the soul that is God's image in man. Externally speaking, the difference between *homo sapiens* and a chimpanzee is only 2.5 percent of the DNA, and some of these 2.5 percent are irrelevant to the essential difference between humans and animals (e.g., genes that determine the amount of hair on the body, etc.). The important difference is the divine image, manifested in the search for truth, as well as in the freedom of choice. Just about all the other talents and abilities we have can also be found in the animal world.

One example for the search for truth is π, the ratio of a circle's circumference to its diameter. π is a transcendental, infinite number. For most purposes it suffices to know that it is 3.14, but some people have calculated not only the tenth number after the dot but also the thousandth, the ten thousandth, the millionth. Why did they do that? There is no practical use; there is not a single thing in the entire cosmos that requires such a degree of precision. People bothered to make such calculations out of this very same desire: to get a tiny bit closer to the truth. We know that we shall never, ever reach it, and yet we try, we make efforts, we strive to reach it.

Such a search is transcendental; it is part of our search for the Absolute.

Here, too, there are people for whom such matters mean nothing, and others — artists and scientists — for whom they are the very center of their lives, people for whom finding yet another tiny bit of truth is an urge, a passion, a craving, an irresistible need. Truth may sometimes be found in things that are totally impractical.

Suppose somebody finds a trans-uranium element whose serial number is 128, which can exist in the world for a thousandth of a second and which probably has no practical value whatsoever; yet such an element would be another part of this so-elusive, so-alluring truth.

So too with Talmud study. Talmud deals with a wide variety of issues — from the very practical (e.g., the minimal size of *tzitzit*, or the size of the piece of leather required for making *tefillin*) through in-depth discussions of opinions that will never serve as the basis for any ruling (e.g., Sumachus' approach to money that is in doubt — Tractate Bava Kamma 46a), to things that have no practical significance whatsoever, things that never were and possibly will never be. Why? Out of the very same desire to reach the truth.

It may sometime happen that things that at one point seemed totally imaginary — such as "a tower in the air" (Sanhedrin 106b), or "sticking two uteri together" (Hullin 70a) — will turn out, a few hundred years later, to be completely realistic and practical (airplanes, surrogate mothers). The halachic decisors who discussed artificial insemination hundreds of years before it became possible did so not because they wanted to know what will happen in such a case, or what could be the practical significance of such a discussion, but because they sought the truth. The ultimate purpose of this kind of study is not the practical outcome, but the truth; what the learner wants is to come close to the other side of reality, so to speak, to God.

This search for God, this inexplicable desire, is what makes us human.

I had a friend who was not a young person and was a rather wild human being, who became a *baal teshuvah*. One day I asked him what made him go in that direction, and he said that it was a verse in the *Book of Job* (14:15), "You would have a desire to (or yearn for) the work of Your hands." If God longs for me, he said, how can I say no?

In his case, it took him 40 years to capitulate; but this yearning of God for the work of His hands — whether I know it or am ignorant of it, whether or not I think about it, whether I believe in it or not — something in me feels that God is telling me, "I miss you, where are you?" Then, knowingly or unknowingly, begins this search, which can take tortuous routes. I believe that whoever is truly a man of science, not a scientific wheeler-dealer, must somehow reach this point of searching for *Truth*.

This feeling of being summoned, of having to search, emerges also from Professor Greene's correspondence with the Rebbe. This correspondence was actually quite bizarre. Greene's first letters to the Rebbe were full of questions, not so much in the realm of philosophy as in natural science, evolution, the time-scale of the universe, how the world evolved, teleology, etc.

And the Rebbe's reply was that he should put on *tefillin*.

This answer drove him nuts, but he began doing that. Then he sent the Rebbe another long series of questions, bigger and more serious than the first, and the Rebbe's reply was that it would be advisable for him to have a kosher kitchen at home. And he did that too.

In this correspondence he asked questions and wanted to receive answers, but those questions were secondary, tertiary, or less, in his order of priorities. What he was looking for first and foremost was the truth. And when he felt he had found a crack through which it was possible to glimpse the truth, he went for it. And if some questions still remained unanswered — so what? The world is full of billions of unanswered, sometimes unanswerable questions.

Some people can dedicate a lifetime to writing three verses that will sound like truth and be true, or to big and small searches, in this world, among the stars, or beyond the stars, as it says (Psalms 139:8), "If I ascend up into heaven, You are there; if I make my bed in the nether-world, behold, You are there." There is no objective way of determining the truth, but we can *feel* the truth. And once that happens, then one says, "This is it! I have touched the absolute, now I must bow down."

It says about Moses that after hearing God's attributes he prostrated himself. Why? Because he saw the *Truth*. When one reaches the point of truth, one ceases to ask and to query. One just bows down. That's what Professor Velvl Greene did.

— Rabbi Adin Even-Israel Steinsaltz

Beersheva, Israel

2012

INTRODUCTION

When I first met the Lubavitcher Rebbe, Rabbi Menachem Mendel Schneerson, he asked if I was familiar with the chasidic principle of *hashgochah protis*, divine providence. *Hashgochah protis*, the Rebbe said, means that everything a person sees or hears is designed by God to bring us closer to God and His Torah.

I knew of the principle, but I did wonder how that could be. Is it possible that every single thing any of us sees or hears during any normal day is really tailor made — individually designed — to bring us closer to God?

Seeing my obvious skepticism, the Rebbe told me a story about *hashgochah protis*, one that came from Rabbi Yisrael Baal Shem Tov, the founder of the chasidic movement.

Back in the Baal Shem Tov's day, even his *chasidim* had their doubts about the extent of *hashgochah protis*. Surely, not *everything* could be the result of divine providence, could it?

One of them offered an example, "When we were walking to *shul*, to synagogue, this morning," he said, "we saw Christians out on the frozen lake, cutting a crucifix out of the ice! What could any Jew possibly learn from that? A crucifix is the antithesis of Judaism! How could God use that sight to teach us anything?"

But think about the ice, the Baal Shem Tov said. Ice is water, and what is more integral to Jewish spirituality than water? It touches every aspect of Jewish life — before a child is conceived, the woman immerses in a *mikvah*, a ritual bath. All through the day, we wash our hands and bless God — when we wake, before we eat, after using the bathroom. In the Torah, there are exhaustive directions given to the Kohen Gadol, the High Priest, about all the water rituals.

And finally, before a body is buried, the last ritual is to wash it.

For a Jew, water is the essence of *kedushah*, holiness. But, the Baal Shem Tov said, when water becomes ice — when it's petrified, frozen, and not moving — then you can cut a crucifix out of it.

Seeing my smile, the Rebbe spoke directly to me. "*Hashgochah protis* is true for every person, everyone who walks in every street, everywhere in the world, every day," he said. "But how much more true is it for you. You're unique! You work in the space program, you're a professor in a medical school. In your lectures, you meet thousands of interesting people. You travel all over the world, and deal with all kinds of things a normal person would never see. Every day you see and hear things that are a very potent source of *hashgochah protis*."

"Why don't you keep a journal?" the Rebbe said. "Nothing elaborate. Just write down a few things at the end of the day, little things you've seen or heard. If you can't see for yourself what the divine message might be, bring it to me and I'll help."

Happily, I took the first part of the Rebbe's advice. I did begin keeping a journal, just writing a few things, notes about some of the things I saw or heard. Although I kept them, sadly, I never brought the journals to the Rebbe. I was concerned about taking up too much of his time.

Today I have 40 years worth of stories, anecdotes, and recorded thoughts — meditations, really — that reflect not only my spiritual growth, but how my work influenced my understanding of Torah, and vice versa. The Rebbe never saw these journals, but now I offer them to you. The book you hold in your hands is a selection of the notes and meanderings that, over the years, I've pondered over, thought about, and jotted down.

Some of the stories are very personal, things that happened to me. Others record events that happened to other people — but when they brought their stories to me, I went off on a mind journey of my own. All of them involve things I saw or heard that caused me to think, consider, and wonder: What was God trying to teach me with this experience? Sometimes I think I see what divine providence intended, sometimes it's still a mystery.

Your coming across this book might be a bit of *hashgochah protis* all by itself.

Perhaps within these pages you'll see the hand of God, somewhere, working in your life as He worked in mine.

Everything a person sees or hears is designed by God to reveal something about Him you need to know. My hope is that somehow, in some way, my stories will join with yours, and together we'll see *hashgochah protis* in action.

— Velvl Greene

Beersheva, Israel

2010

CHAPTER 1

ON THE PATH

There Is God in the World

What's in a Name?

I introduce myself as Velvl, which is a very Yiddish name. It's the name of my Zeide, *zichrono livrachah*, of blessed memory, but I was not named Velvl on my birth certificate. My birth certificate actually says William Greene — that's the way I was called all my life. All my people who knew me then called me Willie. The *goyim* call me Bill, believe it or not. It's a strange thing.

But in the early 1940s, I was in high school, I think, when we heard what was going on in Warsaw, the ghetto. We didn't hear about the death camps, we just heard about what was going on in Warsaw. A number of us responded differently; the kids in our HaBonim movement, some of them came to school wearing yellow flags, yellow badges.

I did something very personal: I actually changed my name officially in court from William to Velvl. Even in Israel, where they want to call you Zev or something, my name is Velvl. It was a juvenile kind of reaction, but that's where we were.

3

FIRST IMPRESSION

*B*ack in the early 1960s, Rabbi Moshe Feller was the *shaliach*, the emissary, that the Rebbe sent to Minnesota. His job was to bring Jews closer to *Yiddishkeit*. Rabbi Feller had heard about me and wanted to meet with me face to face. At the time, I was doing research for NASA as well as for the Army Biological Laboratory. I worked in a very, very secure laboratory. There was no access for anybody without high clearance.

He tried to call and make an appointment, but I told him it was impossible. When I first got a call from him, I knew, a guy with a black hat comes to Minneapolis — how many guys with black hats are there in Minneapolis? — so I knew he's a *meshulach*, he's a representative, he's coming to get money.

So I told him on the phone, "You don't have to come — I'll send a check." And he said, "I don't need a check." That's the first time he said that, and the last time he said it, "I don't need a check, I want to see you." I said, "Rabbi, I'll give you twice as much." I thought ah, I'm going to give him $36 instead of $18. He said, "I must speak to you, it's a matter of extreme importance."

Believe it or not, I arranged for him to come.

He came into my office. This is a little Jew with a black hat, a beard, two big guards on both sides of him with guns. I saw that and my heart just, you know — I was sympathetic to him, even though I knew he was there for money or something else, whatever gig he had.

So I asked him to sit down and we talked. I said, "You're a nice guy, I'm gonna tell you how to be successful. The first thing you got to do is trim the beard a little bit. Look like a *mensch*. Get out of that

4

black suit, you look like an undertaker." I was giving him good advice. He was listening.

And then he looked out the window — this is important — he looked out the window and he looked at me. He said, "Excuse me, I've got to do something." I said, "Well, the bathroom is over there." No. He got up, he took a cord from his pocket, he tied it around his waist, and he started to shake back and forth.

What is he doing? It's not Rosh Hashanah and it's not Yom Kippur. Is he praying? It's the middle of the afternoon and there is no one telling him what page to be on. After all, this was my job as a Reform rabbi, to tell you what page you're on. There was no one telling him what page to be on. And most of all, I was no longer in control. He's in *my* office, he asked for an appointment, and he's ignoring me. He's facing the window and he's shaking.

When he was finished, he sat down again. I said, "Rabbi Feller, the interview is over; you've insulted me. You came for an appointment with me and all of a sudden you're doing some mumbo-jumbo." And then he said the key words. He said, "What I came for was very, very important, but what I had to do now was even more important."

If you want to know what changed, if you want to talk about the word *epiphany* — that happened there. Now I know he was *davening Minchah*, the afternoon prayer, and he had to do it before the sun went down — and that was more important than even what he came for. Now that is dedication, and that impressed me.

Lesson from Life

A young man came from a wealthy, but not well-educated, Jewish family. When he was still a boy, he was sent off to a *yeshivah*, a Jewish school, by his father, certainly an excellent decision.

The boy stayed and studied — one year, two years, five years, 10, 15. One day the young man was home, and his father started to wonder.

"So, Yaakov," he began. "You've been studying in that expensive *yeshivah* for 15 years now. What have you learned?"

The young man paused, and then said, "I've learned that there is a God in the world."

The father was astounded. "*Nu?* Fifteen years of education, and that's all you've learned? That God is in the world? Any idiot can know that!"

The father called to Mary, a non-Jewish woman who'd worked for the family for many years. "Mary," he said. "Who made heaven and earth?"

"God did," she answered promptly.

"See?" said the father, turning back to his son. "There's Mary — a poor, uneducated, non-Jewish woman. And yet she says there's a God."

"It's not the same, Papa," the son said. "Mary *says* it. But I *know* it."

Saying something and *knowing* it are not the same thing.

THE CHALLENGE

*A*t the time that I met Rabbi Feller, I was a young professor who was already sending his daughter to the Torah Academy, who was interested in Jewish things, and who was growing in his field, who was becoming well known in the community. I was raising money for Israel Bonds and for the United Jewish Appeal and I was on the board of the Talmud Torah.

And one day, Rabbi Feller simply said to me, "You don't know *Yiddishkeit*, you don't know Torah."

I said, "Of course I do — I was a Reform rabbi for two years."

He said, "You don't know Torah."

So I said, "Well, how do I ...?"

He said, "I'll teach you, we'll learn together."

And we started learning together. I was up to the challenge.

I trust that everything is in order, and insofar as a Jew

is concerned, "in order" means that things are not stationary,

but are progressing steadily.

— Rabbi Menachem Mendel Schneerson, 1978

TASTE AND SEE

A favorite maxim among my chasidic friends is the quotation from Psalms, "Taste and see that the Lord is good," which they explain as follows: No matter how one appraises a morsel of food, no matter how well one describes it and discusses it or analyzes it or inspects it, one doesn't feel its flavor until one tastes it.

This is why the *Chasidim* are such activists with respect to encouraging everyone to perform the *mitzvot*. This is why they conduct their phenomenally successful live-and-learn programs. Put on *tefillin* and you will know what *tefillin* are. Observe a Shabbos and you will discern the beauty of Shabbos. Taste and see — the philosophy will become more meaningful.

The Next Step

The book *Kiddush HaShem* by Sholem Asch describes the Jews in the 1648 holocaust of Chelminitzki and the Ukraine, and how there were Jews who would give up their life rather than convert. These were our people — this wasn't in Spain, this was our great, great grandparents.

One of the arguments we were having in our Reconstructionist group was: Are there still people around who would give up their life for something as ephemeral as belief in God? Normal people, not crazies.

When I saw Rabbi Feller *davening Minchah*, I picked up the phone and called Gail. I said we got one; there is a guy sitting in my office right now who would be one of those people who would give up his life. I've got to bring him to the study group, I have to let people see him. So he came to our house and he met our friends. And so this was the next step.

We had met people who sent their kids to Torah Academy, but here was a man who lived this life. This man represented Jewish history. He represented the kind of people I had admired without knowing I admired them. It was alive — he wasn't a living fossil.

He was an expert in baseball. He knew all the scores of all the games. He knew all the records of all the pitchers. And he knew Torah.

LESSON NUMBER ONE

The first meeting with the Rebbe was going to be at 10 o'clock at night. This is the way it worked: You came at 10 o'clock, and the Rebbe spent the whole evening meeting people. I was the first one on the list. There was a whole line of people coming. I was the new boy on the block.

I was walking up and down Kingston Avenue, which is where the Rebbe's world headquarters is, and I noticed something — I should have known it, I'm a professor — everyone is wearing a hat. I'm walking around bareheaded. I didn't even have a yarmulke. I didn't think about it. But I needed a hat. Everyone is wearing a hat. Where do you get a hat at 9 o'clock at night in New York? So I asked around, are there any stores open? Someone said, well, there is a lady …

Maryasha Garelik was her name. She was the queen of Chabad. She was the mother and grandmother and great-grandmother of so many Chabad people. And she, at her age, even then she was old — she was over 100 years old when she passed on — but she was working then. She had a remnants sale. People would give her old clothes; she would sell them and give the money to the *yeshivah*. The man said she's always open.

So I went out, went down a couple steps, and I found her, Maryasha. I said, "I need a hat." "Oh," she said, "I got just the thing for you. Here is a hat. Look, it's a beautiful hat. Thirty-five cents."

I looked at this hat. First of all, the hat was funny colored. I don't know what the original color was but it's lost in history; it goes back to the dinosaurs. You don't believe in dinosaurs? This hat is proof that the dinosaurs existed. I think it was made from dinosaurs.

What is more, there were certain bits of color in the hat. The Torah talks about a spiritual malady called leprosy — not only of people and of buildings, but leprosy of fabrics. This hat had it. It had red spots and green spots, which I, as a microbiologist, know are fungi, mold.

But that's the hat she wanted me to buy. It's 9 o'clock at night, I have an appointment with the Rebbe at 10 o'clock. I bought the hat, thirty-five cents. I put the hat on. It's getting dark outside. All right, protective coloration, I'm wearing the hat.

I went in to 770, the headquarters, and Rabbi Groner met me. He looked at that hat and he didn't know whether to take me seriously. But he is trained to deal with fools, all sorts of people come in, so he let me come in. He knocked on the door and said, "Professor Greene is here." The Rebbe got up, walked to the door, took me by the elbow, held the chair for me, I sat down.

The first question the Rebbe had for me, in the first time I actually had an audience with him privately, was what language we should speak. I told him that I could speak Yiddish, and it would be more comfortable for me to speak to the Rebbe in Yiddish than any other language. So that was fine; we spoke Yiddish. We established rapport.

The second question he had, "Do you have a yarmulke?"

A funny question — I'm wearing a hat, the Rebbe was wearing a hat, Rabbi Groner was wearing a hat, Rabbi Krinsky was wearing a hat, everyone was wearing a hat. So I come in wearing a hat, and the Rebbe asks me, "Do you have a yarmulke?"

I said, "No, I don't have a yarmulke." It was the second question and the second answer: "No, I don't have a yarmulke."

So the Rebbe said in Yiddish, "Maybe I have one here in my

drawer." He rummaged around in his desk to see if there was a yarmulke. Yeah, he found a yarmulke. He said, "Here, take this yarmulke and take off the hat."

So I asked the question — I said, "Rebbe, you're wearing a hat, everyone is wearing a hat ..."

He said, "Please take off the hat." He said, "I can't say a serious thing to you while you're wearing that hat."

So I took off the hat. And I learned my first lesson. People ask, "What did you learn from the Rebbe?" Two things: Number one, don't make an ass of yourself. Number two, if you have to deal with an ass, be nice to him.

TEFILLIN IN DACHAU

S omeone smuggled a pair of *tefillin* into Dachau. It was a rarity. There were people there who really needed to put on *tefillin*, and the man who had them rented them out. What did he charge? A crust of bread. Maybe someone gets a crust of bread a day and he'd pay that so he could put on the *tefillin*. Or maybe he'd give up his plate of soup, or offer to do a dirty job, so he could put on the *tefillin*.

When it was over, the man who owned the *tefillin* was accused of being a profiteer. He had a monopoly on *tefillin*, and he took from other people everything they had, to the extent that they endangered their own lives.

I don't mean to make a point for him. I've got enough of a capitalist strain in me that I recognize how it worked — that he had to sell the thing to save his life.

I prefer to tell the story from the perspective of how many people gave up their crust of bread in order to have a chance to put on *tefillin*.

The guy who rented them — that's human nature. But giving up your crust of bread for the privilege of putting on the *tefillin* — that is not human nature.

TRADITION

It was early summer when I first met Rabbi Feller and the other *Chasidim*. I said to them, "Why are you wearing the clothing of some Polish noblemen of the 15th century? It's hot outside. If I had any kind of sense, I'd take my shirt off."

Rabbi Feller said, "We do this because it is our tradition."

"Right," I said, "but tradition can be manifested in ways that aren't so ..."

He said, "But this is who I am."

Later that afternoon, there was a commencement at the University of Minnesota. All of the faculty, several thousand, were dressed in caps and gowns. This was June, and some of the gowns had fur on them, they were very heavy. They all wore hats, and these long, long gowns.

People came to the ceremony, and my God, you could hear the drama, the Academic Overture showing this is the academic tradition. And so, why were these academic idiots dressed up like this in June?

THE THRESHOLD

*A*t the first meeting with the Rebbe, in 1963, he gave me the marching order, the rules. He said, "You must help Rabbi Feller. You appear to me as a man of the community, as someone who is a little more established, a professor and so forth, and Rabbi Feller is there; you must help him."

So that's what we did for the rest of our life, basically.

I was impressed. The man represented to me as a *navi*, as a prophet. In fact, we have a book by Rabbi Abraham Joshua Heschel called *The Prophets*, in which he is trying to ascertain if there is a unifying characteristic of all the different *neviim*. Each one was from a different time, they lived in a different period, they had different personalities. Some of them were rich and some of them were prominent; some of them were just peasants, farmers. Heschel put together some of the characteristics of a prophet.

Chaim Nachman Bialik also wrote Yiddish poems about who is a *navi*. When I saw the Rebbe, my first impression was from the heart. As a little boy, 10, 11 years old, in the Peretz Shul in Winnipeg, I memorized a poem by Bialik. In Hebrew it was called *"Im Yesh Et Nafshecha L'Daat"*; in Yiddish, *"Oib Dyn Neshama Vill Dergayn Dem Kvall"*; in English, "If Your Soul Wants to Get to the Bottom Source."

In it Bialik writes about the history of the Jewish people. What gave the Jews the strength to withstand all of the libels and the punishments and the suffering and the wandering and the banishment and still remain who they are? In his poem Bialik says, *"Oy bruder, oib vilst veesen fun dos altz,"* if you want to know where they got the strength to put out their knife to meet their heart and jump into the fires of the Spanish Inquisition, if you want to know, he says, *"Bais medrash kumt,"* come to the synagogue. And there you will see, on a long winter night, an old man studying the Talmud of thousands of years ago; there you will see a man who can hardly read, pouring out his heart, saying the psalms in *Tehillim;* there you will see 10 people *davening,* praying, because they brought down the *Shechinah* upon them, they brought down the countenance of God to rest on them.

Bialik says if you see this, then you should know — listen to the words in Yiddish, *"Dos shtayst du aifen shvell fun unzer lebben,"* you're standing on the threshold of our life, *"Un zehn dayn oigen dee neshama,"* your eyes are looking into the Jewish soul.

Standing there in 770, in December 1963, all I could think of was this poem. This is the threshold. This is the Jewish soul. Honestly, I recognized that poem. I didn't need anymore propaganda. I didn't need anymore. This was for me.

THE LAST ONES ALIVE

Thee was a meeting in Warsaw in June of 1962 between the Russian Academy of Science and the American National Academy of Science. I was chosen as a delegate to this meeting. We were going to write what we call the *Planetary Quarantine Agreement* because we were ready to do exploration on other planets and we wanted to make sure we wouldn't bring any of our terrestrial or earth bacteria to other planets.

While I was negotiating with the Russians how to disinfect the spacecraft and how to sterilize the hardware, my wife, Gail, was wandering around Jewish Warsaw. There was no Jewish Warsaw. There was destruction. Where the ghetto used to be was still a pile of rubble, just mounds of gravel and dirt. No map. But we had a book written by Leon Uris called *Mila 18* and on the back of that book is a hand-drawn map of where the ghetto was. Gail used that map to walk through the streets and identify this street and that street. It made a tremendous impression on her.

She came back to the hotel one afternoon crying, bitterly crying, hysterically crying. She sat down on the bed and I couldn't calm her. I didn't know what happened. And she fixed me with a look that I'll never forget. She said, "I don't care what you say, Velvl, when we get home, I'm going to make my kitchen kosher."

I laughed. She didn't know I had the faintest idea what a kosher kitchen was. I at least remembered my grandmother's kitchen, which was kosher.

I said, "It's too hard, it's too expensive, they'll cheat you." The way I first thought of them — they're kosher butchers, they're going to cheat you. She said, "I don't care." She said, "We're the last ones alive and if I don't make a kosher kitchen, our kids won't be Jewish."

Rabbi Feller is a sweet guy. Most *shluchim*, emissaries, are sweet people. They do things, anything. But no one had ever asked him to make a kitchen kosher before. He didn't even know that we didn't have a kosher kitchen.

He came into our house and he saw what was in our refrigerator. It was a scene, it should be a movie. He stood with his back against the refrigerator, guarding it, and he said, "Do you eat that stuff?"

"Yeah, we eat it."

"Don't touch it, don't touch it! Get me tape, get me tape!" He wanted to tape the refrigerator.

"Rabbi?"

"Don't touch it, don't touch it!"

That was another beginning. Our house became kosher long before I became kosher. I'll admit it now, I still ate in the campus club. Gail made the kitchen kosher because of this crazy idea that we're the only ones left, and if our kitchen isn't kosher, we won't have Jewish grandchildren.

The Favor

eople actually came to services to hear Gail sing. She was the lead soprano in the choir of a Conservative synagogue, and she is a wonderful singer.

Moshe Feller came to my office once; this time he didn't sit down and *daven*, he was in a bit of a fluster. He said, "Gail can't sing; it's not nice for Gail to sing on Rosh Hashanah and Yom Kippur at the Conservative temple. In fact, we have a problem."

I told him, "We don't have a problem — you have a problem. I'm not going to touch this."

So he said, "How about if I were to pay your fare to New York, you and Gail, and you go ask the Rebbe whether she should sing."

I said, "Don't be an idiot; I know that the Rebbe is going to say no. I mean, if you say no, the Rebbe will certainly say no."

"But you go ask him yourself."

I said, "You're going to pay for a trip for us, no strings attached, no guarantees? OK, fine."

There is only one problem. This was in Elul, the month before Rosh Hashanah. Gail was supposed to sing on Rosh Hashanah. The Rebbe does not have audiences with private people in Elul. This is the time when Jews prepare for the new year, for the coronation. This is the beginning of the Days of Awe, when we start saying *Selichos*, special penitential prayers. The Rebbe doesn't have time for things like that.

Nonetheless, Rabbi Feller arranged that we would have a private audience with the Rebbe, not only during Elul, but in the middle of the day, which is very rare, and Rabbi Feller paid the fare. I don't know where he got the money.

So Gail and I arrived at the airport and were picked up by the Rebbe's secretary, Rabbi Krinsky, who drove us in the Cadillac. We went in. When he knocked at the door and said Professor and Mrs. Greene are here, in Yiddish, the Rebbe got up from his chair and walked over to the door.

The Rebbe opened the door and he said hello to Gail and he took me by the elbow and led us to his desk, where he stood and held a chair for Gail to sit in — a French gentleman all the way. And then he stood behind me and held a chair for me to sit down, and then we talked to him.

At this first meeting that Gail and I had with the Rebbe, we sat for an hour in Elul, we talked about many, many things. The Rebbe wanted to know about our children, above all. He wanted Gail to describe each of them. At that time, we only had three. The Rebbe looked at the pictures of our children and he pointed to the little boy and said, "Did he have his hair cut yet?"

Gail said, "Well, of course. What do you think, we're primitive? A little boy, civilized, should have a haircut." He was almost three.

So the Rebbe said, "No, no," and he smiled. "You should ask Rabbi Feller what we mean by an *upsherinish*." He said it's a custom among *Chasidim* to wait until the third birthday and then to cut the hair.

He said, "But you've already cut the hair, so do me a favor" — again a favor, the Rebbe never asked us or demanded anything from me except to give reports, but everything else was a favor — "do me a favor, wait from now until Chanukah and don't cut his hair for the next two months or three months. Then make a big party and invite all the Jewish children from the neighborhood. Remember to buy a lot of presents for your daughters so they shouldn't be jealous, so they should also enjoy the party, and take pictures of the little boy while he is having his hair cut, and send me that picture."

So that's the Rebbe — always with the children, always a *brachah* with the children.

Where children are concerned, every benefit accruing them in

childhood is multiplied as they grow into adulthood.

— *Rabbi Menachem Mendel Schneerson, 1964*

THE ANSWER

A set of English bone china was given to us as a present from my sisters when we got married. It was the most expensive thing we ever owned. It was nearly as expensive as our car at that time. It was an heirloom. It was beautiful. It was our pride. It was up there in the breakfront.

The dishes were made of clay — maybe porcelain, which is still clay — and according to the Torah, this becomes contaminated with non-kosher food. You can't use it and you can't clean it and you can't burn it; you have to throw it away, break it. It's *treif*, non-kosher.

Rabbi Feller might have been a naive *yeshivah bachur*, a student who interrupted a conversation with me to *daven* at *Minchah* time, but he knew very well the problem with porcelain. When Gail asked, "What are we going to do with these, Rabbi? Should I get a pot of hot water and boil it?" — he said, "No, no, no, don't boil it. There is something special about china and I'm going to have to ask the question in New York from a rabbi who really knows how to make this kosher."

Rabbi Feller was exaggerating a little bit — there ain't no such thing, unless he was going to ask a Reform rabbi like me. To make a long story short, he went to New York but he forgot to ask. The man wasn't there the next time. And then he said that's just an opinion and we've got to get a better expert. This dragged on for years.

"Don't touch these dishes. You're not eating from them?" he asked.

"No, no, no."

"I'll find out — but don't use them. Don't use them."

In the meantime, we started practicing *taharat hamishpachah*, the laws of family purity, which means Gail started going to the *mikvah*. And we started having miscarriages. Gail would get pregnant and lose the baby, sometimes early, sometimes late. Four times in a row. After having three lovely, healthy children and then starting to go to the *mikvah* and doing everything right, this is what we get? So the question of the dishes was put aside for a while because we had other things to worry about.

Then, after the fourth miscarriage, I came home and Gail said, "I think I found the problem."

She said, "I took our dishes and gave them to our neighbor, a non-Jewish woman, and she gave me $50 for them, and I went and bought a *shaitel*, a wig that an observant woman wears, with the $50."

When we were in England, the ladies of the Chabad women's movement heard the story and bought her a set of English bone china even better than the last. And from then on we had, *Baruch Hashem*, thank God, another two healthy children.

SNEAKING INTO RUSSIA

I n 1982, people in Chabad were being arrested and put in jail. We got a message that three professors in Russia were falling under the influence of Chabad and wanted to become a little more observant, but they had a tremendous barrier because of the science–Torah conflict. In Russia, they were taught that religion and Torah are old and primitive and belong in the past.

I had another *yechidus*, a meeting, with the Rebbe, and he asked if I could arrange legally to find some kind of scientific meeting or convention behind the Iron Curtain that would justify getting a visa and taking my wife to Russia. He said there's a fund that would pay for the trip. It's called *Lishkat Ezrat Achim*, a Chabad fund that was raised during this time to provide the Jews in Russia with the wherewithal, with *tefillin* and prayerbooks and *talleisim*. So I found a meeting that was going to be in Russia and I got an official visa for me and Gail to go.

We had a stop-off in London, where we had once spent three months, so we had a lot of friends. The man who was going to brief us on exactly what we had to do was Rabbi Shmuel Lew, who happened to be Mrs. Feller's brother.

Every day, Rabbi Lew would show us pictures of people — these were trustworthy, these were not trustworthy — and we had to memorize the pictures. It's like cloak-and-dagger work, it's a real spy story. The day before we were supposed to go, he came to our room and asked to see our suitcases. He said, "Take everything out. For you, one suit for Shabbos, one suit for the week, that's it. For Gail, you can take a little more. I need the space."

"What do you mean you need the space?"

He said, "We have orders for things. There is a *sofer*, a scribe, in Russia who is writing, who makes *tefillin*. He needs leather straps, he needs ink, he needs parchment paper, or *klaf*, to write this on. There is someone in Kiev who wants a dictionary of the Talmud. There is someone who needs *chalav Yisrael*, extra kosher milk, for her baby."

The most unique item we were to carry was a divorce decree. A Russian woman had been deserted by her husband. They'd received a Soviet divorce, but afterward, she'd become observant and wanted a *get*, a religious divorce, so she could marry again. The woman had contacted the Rebbe, and now the documents needed to be delivered to the woman's rabbi in Moscow.

So Rabbi Lew emptied all our bags and filled them with this contraband material to bring into Russia in the middle of the period when they investigate you. And we were going to meet with Russians, which they don't want you to do.

Finally, on the morning Rabbi Lew was going to take us to the airport, he arrived with four pairs of Lubavitch *tzitzit*, the little undershirt that Chabad men wear with the four fringes attached to it, to fulfill the *mitzvah* of wearing a fringed garment. All religious men wear it, but Chabad wears a special kind — they wear woolen ones. This was August; it's hot. I said to Shmuel Lew, "I can't put them into the suitcase; how many pairs of *tzitzit* does a person need?"

He said, "Oh no, you don't put them in the suitcase, you wear them."

I said, "You mean wear one, two, three, four pairs of *tzitzit*? Look at me, Shmuel, I really have enough girth. I put this on, I'll be rolling. They'll look at me." Rabbi Lew turned to me and said, "And one looks normal?"

The truth of the matter is we took them. I wore two and packed two. We took the straps that the *tefillin* are made of and used that to tie our suitcases together. Gail brought the ink for the *sofer* in her cosmetic bag, it looked like mascara. When it came to the divorce papers — written in Hebrew — she concocted a ready explanation: "I study music. This is a very rare copy of ancient Yemenite music. I don't even understand it myself yet."

When we got to Moscow, we had to go through customs, where they open the suitcases. Everyone opens their suitcase completely and they go through it all, especially people who look like I do, a beard and a *kippah*, a yarmulke. We were worried but we had our story.

Gail had to go to the bathroom. Moscow airport is built like most everything in Russia — the doors don't fit, so she couldn't open the door. So she was sitting there like in a prison, the door was floor to ceiling, there was no place to crawl through. I was out there waiting, getting nervous, with all these bags, obviously attracting an awful lot of attention, and I'm afraid maybe they abducted Gail, maybe they're sweating her out someplace. It was not a pleasant moment.

Finally, some woman who needed to get in the bathroom pulled the door open and released Gail. She came out to me, she was crying, she was so worried.

So we started taking the bags over and just as we were getting to the customs inspector, another plane landed and hundreds of people got off and were all standing in line behind us pushing and shoving. The customs officer asked Gail, "Do you have any jewelry?" Gail said, "Yes." And she started taking out every little pair of earrings, every ring. Meanwhile, the crowd is getting longer and longer behind us. So the woman said, "Is that all? Go! Close it!"

So I picked up these two heavy suitcases and ran through the airport like I was flying. And this is the way we got into Russia.

Bear in mind that the ways of G-d are inscrutable, but always

good, since He is the Essence of Goodness, and it is in the

nature of the Good to do good — however difficult it may

sometimes seem to comprehend. Yet it is not at all surprising

that a human being should not be able to understand the ways

of G-d; on the contrary, it is quite easy to see why a human

being should not be able to understand the ways of G-d,

for how can a created being understand the Creator?

We must, therefore, be strong in our trust in G-d, and let

nothing discourage us or cause any depression, G-d forbid.

As a matter of fact, the stronger the Bitochon (confidence) in

G-d and His benevolence, the sooner comes the time when

this becomes plain even to human eyes.

— Rabbi Menachem Mendel Schneerson, 1970

A LITTLE CRAZY

I t always surprises me when people come to hear me lecture, to listen to what I have to say. I always ask them, "Why are you here? What are you doing, anyway? You came to listen to me? There are great rabbis out there you could listen to! There are little kids who know more Torah than I do. For that matter, there are movies and baseball games! You must be crazy, to be here!"

Maybe we're all a little crazy, when you think of it.

The conscious state of a Jew can be affected by external factors

to the extent of inducing states of mind and even behavior

which is contrary to his subconscious, which is the Jew's

essential nature. When the external pressures are removed,

it does not constitute a change or transformation of his

essential nature, but, on the contrary, merely the reassertion

of his innate and true character.

— *Rabbi Menachem Mendel Schneerson, 1965*

THE HOT DOG STAND

Once a week, Rabbi Feller and I would learn together. We were getting to know each other better, and he asked if the next time I took a trip on a plane I'd order a kosher meal.

I looked at him and I said, "Why? You know I don't keep kosher." He told me, "First of all, I want you to keep kosher." He never insisted on it, but he did say it wouldn't hurt me to keep kosher.

"Second of all," he said, "when I order a kosher meal, they never have it. So I figure that maybe if two of us were ordering it, maybe they'd think it was a mass movement, and maybe we'd get somewhere." So he said, "Do me a favor and order one."

Would you refuse a guy a favor?

I called the airline office, and they said OK, it's on our record, we have your order, it's done.

I flew very frequently and sometimes the stewardesses recognized me. The flight took an hour and a half, Minneapolis to Chicago. They started serving breakfast. It was scrambled eggs and sausage and coffee. It smelled good, I was hungry. She came to give it to me, and I looked up in shock, "But I ordered a kosher meal!" And she looked at me — I think she recognized me already, I ate the same thing last week, two weeks ago. She said, "I'll check up front."

There's a clue, if you don't know it by now. When they say they'll check up front, forget it. If you think you're going to have breakfast, it ain't there. If they had it, they would have served it first. That's what they do. They serve it first, get those special ones out of the way quickly.

She came back, "Dr. Greene, maybe I can help you."

"All right," I said.

"Maybe if you move the sausage from over here to over here..."

Well, it was perfectly good logic, but I took umbrage.

"I ordered a kosher meal! And you're trying to get me to be *treif*, to be unkosher?" I asked. "We have a heritage for 3,000 years."

It was all a sham. I was annoyed, and I told myself it was the airline's fault anyway. They apologized, but there I was, hungry, mad. Hungry and mad. I was mad at myself for being an idiot. I was mad at the airline, certainly. And I was mad at Rabbi Feller, who put me through this torturous starvation process.

I was mad at God. I mean, there I was, in His territory, at 23,000 feet. This is where the *Chasidim* were teaching me that God can do anything. I called out, "He can do everything! And He can't even get a meal on Northwest Airlines?"

We landed at Midway Airport, and about every 10 meters there was a different kind of stand. This was Chicago. There were bratwurst, liverwurst, all the wursts you're not supposed to eat. The place smelled like great, big, jubilee barbecue, delicious. I was hungry. It wasn't my fault that they didn't have a meal on board. I'd done my part, I was absolutely free of sin. I was pissed off.

So I whipped to the phone. I went right past all these hot dog stands. The first thing I had to do before I ate a hot dog was to call Rabbi Feller and chew him out. I dropped a dime, I reversed the charges.

"Hello, Rabbi Feller?"

"Yes."

"This is Velvl."

He said, "Yes? How was it?"

I said, "I didn't get my meal. I'm hungry. And what's more, I'm surrounded by hot dog stands. I had to walk by hot dog stands to call you, and there you see how bad off I am."

He said, "Do me one more favor?"

"Yeah?"

"Walk past the next hot dog stand."

When I came back to Minnesota, he said, "I want to talk to you about this."

He said, "According to Rambam, the whole world is on a balance beam, every person. The next thing you as an individual do is either going to make it go up or down. The next thing you do will have an impact on it. Because everyone contributes to how this balance beam moves. The fact that you walked by a hot dog stand and didn't eat it, and that you were hungry and justifiably annoyed, you could have brought *Moshiach*, the Messiah, at that particular moment. You should know, that's what you could have done. And the rest of your life is going to be walking by hot dog stands."

PLUGGING IN

*A*t the age of 38, I got my first *tefillin*. Rabbi Feller brought them to me from New York. I didn't pray every day, but Rabbi Feller said that's irrelevant, I should put them on every day, in the daytime.

I became quite obsessed with putting on these *tefillin* every day, wherever I was. And I've heard exactly the same thing from other *baalei teshuvah*, Jews who are becoming more observant, when they get their *tefillin*. The biggest problem is to find a place to put them on. I heard a similar story about a rabbi in Russia. The sun was going down, and he hadn't put them on yet. So he rented a room in a house of ill repute, where they wouldn't ask any questions, and he'd have a private room to put them on.

You become very, very obsessed with it.

An analogy of this story is: We bought a sophisticated piece of equipment, an instrument, and we turned it on. Nothing worked. We called in an engineer from the company. He checked it out, he looked at the fuses, he checked and he looked.

Finally, one of the graduate students saw it — we hadn't plugged it in!

Similarly, a Jew must be "plugged in" before he can start functioning. Regardless of his complexity and sophistication, regardless of his wealth and learning and occupation and involvement, he must take the first step and connect himself to the Power Supply with his *tefillin*. When the "plug" is connected, the power flows, and the "experiment" can start. The instrument is operational.

The Seamless Garment

In the tractate Shekalim, which discusses the gathering of the *shekel* and what the money is used for, there's an interesting sidebar on the clothes the high priest must wear when he goes into the room in the Holy Temple where the *shekalim* are kept. The Talmud says his clothes can't have any seams. No pockets. He can't wear *tefillin* in that room. In these days, he couldn't wear a watch. He doesn't wear shoes.

Why? Not so much because he's going to steal, but in the future, if he becomes poor, then people will say, "Oh, it's punishment because of what he stole." And if he becomes rich, the people will say, "It's because of what he stole."

Anyone who is working with public funds is under suspicion. This is in the Talmud. This goes way back, way back to Moshe Rebbenu, Moses. The Kohen, the high priest, must avoid suspicion at all costs, even down to the kind of clothes he wears when he's counting money, so a coin will not accidentally slide into a pocket or a cuff.

We presume the Kohen is an honest person. This is the Jewish definition of *transparency*, to never create a situation in which suspicion is aroused. We say, "Let us find favor in the eyes of God and man." The Golden Rule is to behave in such a fashion that we find favor in the eyes of God — obviously, we have to follow the rules — but to also find favor in the eyes of men.

It means never doing anything that actually arouses suspicion. It's a story for Israel. If you're in a public position, wear a seamless garment.

COMMON LANGUAGE

A couple of years ago, I was *davening* at a pickup minyan at the Kotel, the Western Wall. Of course, most of the *minyans* are pickups, only a few are prearranged. The guy leading, the *baal tefillah*, was from one of the religious *kibbutzim*. He had short pants, sandals, a big *tallit*, with a gun strapped to his waist under the *tallit*.

This guy was *davening* with a very Sephardic accent; he was a real Israeli, born and bred. And he was emphasizing the words carefully.

We came to the *Birkat Kohanim*, the Priestly Blessing. As it happened, there wasn't a Kohen in our *minyan*, but one guy said, "I know that guy over there, he's a Kohen." So they asked, and sure enough, the Kohen comes back, takes off his shoes, steps up onto a little platform, dons the *tallit*, puts out his hands.

You know the way it works: The *baal tefillah* recites the words very softly, under his breath, and the Kohen repeats it, saying the Aharonic blessing back loudly.

In the blessing, the *baal tefillah* — the *kibbutznik* — gets to the second verse. "*Ya-air*," he starts out. He said it very clearly, in the Israeli *sabra*, Sephardic pronunciation.

But the Kohen repeated it his way. What he said was, "*You-wa-iaiiire*."

The *baal tefillah* listened to that, and of course he's the one who has to judge whether it was said properly or not, and he didn't think so. So he repeated it again,

"*Ya-air*," he said again, even more clearly this time.

And again, the Kohen repeated what he heard, "*You-waiaiiire*."

The *baal tefillah* tried one more time, this time slapping his hand on the table for emphasis, "YA-AIR!"

The Kohen said in Yiddish, "I said it already. I said it."

It was a beautiful example: Here we are, people *davening* together, doing exactly what it says in the Torah: "These are the words with which you should bless the Jewish people," but nowhere in the Torah does it say how to pronounce it.

So the *sabra kibbutznik* Sephardic *baal tefillah* said, "*Ya-air,*" but the Ashkenazi Kohen heard, "*You-waiaiiire,*" which was what he repeated.

This is one of the things we really have to understand, if we're going to build a community here in Israel. One says "*Ya-air*" and the other "*You-waiaiiire*" — but it's the same word. Exactly the same word.

THE MUSIC OF EXISTENCE

Looking at the complexity of an orchestral score, one wonders, "Who wrote all this stuff?" It wasn't Mozart — he didn't write all that. The composer simply writes a set of notes, maybe putting in a little harmony, but basically, it's just a line of music. In order for an orchestra to play it, someone has to write out all the parts: This is for the violin, this is for the bass.

Then my imagination takes over. What would happen if the guy playing the violin decided to play the trombone music instead? What if someone else decides to play the written music as his own muse dictates — to heck with the written score? He's going to improvise! Won't that be interesting?! What if everyone in the orchestra decided they're bored with that particular music?

What you have is a holy mess.

Maybe this could be the answer to the whole question of diversity. In this world, there's a whole bunch of diverse people and diverse things, too. Everything has DNA, but some of that DNA turns out to be trees, while other DNA is a whale. Some of it is people, other is cockroaches.

But let's just take people: Within that category, some are men, some are women. Some are young men, some are old men. Because of the nature of nature, there are some things young men can do that old men can't do. And quite the contrary, too: Maybe, when the Composer wrote the music of existence, He scored the music in such a way that this one part is for old men, and that other part is only for young men.

That's why you have 136 people in the orchestra: The Composer wants to hear a piece of music that has a lot of different instruments.

So to create His harmony, He writes in that He wants this note from this instrument right now, and the note from that other instrument just a beat later. Some notes are written for young men, some for old. Some for women, some for men.

And now a terrible thing has happened: We've just left political correctness behind.

Am I actually suggesting that women might be orchestrated by the Composer to play different notes than men? But hey — I'm just looking at the way it was scored. If it takes a certain number of chromosomes to have the ability to give birth to a baby, I don't think that others, with a different chromosome count, will ever be scored to play the note of baby-birthing. Some of us men might want to do that with all our hearts, but it's not going to be possible. The music just wasn't written that way.

There is a limit, isn't there? We all have our particular freedoms, we have the right to do a great many things. It isn't necessarily smart to do some of them — a violinist who claims the freedom to play trombone music isn't going to get very far in the orchestral world.

Maybe the most important freedom of all is whether to join the orchestra in the first place. But once you join, once you're in the orchestra, you have to play the score the conductor is conducting.

Quite honestly, when they all play together — at the right time, all with the right music, all following the conductor's baton — the music is exquisite.

Maybe that's what *Moshiach*'s Orchestra will sound like: every instrument playing its own part, in exactly the way the Composer wrote, in exactly the way He wanted to hear it. Every instrument playing individually, all together.

CLOTHES DON'T MAKE THE MAN

Rabbi Salanter lived several hundred years ago. Someone came to him and complained that there were members of his congregation who cheat in business.

They wear black hats, they *daven* three times a day, they cheat in business. They're scoundrels. How do you reconcile that with Judaism, with Orthodoxy?

He said, "Yes, I've had that problem. I have people in my congregation who wear black hats and they eat ham. They *daven* three times a day and on Shabbat they do all sorts of things."

They said, "But if he eats ham and he works on Shabbat, then he's not Orthodox."

Exactly.

That's the end of the story. Wearing a black hat and belonging to this congregation does not make you a religious Jew.

Why do we assume that the mark of the observant Jew is that he goes to this synagogue, and wears these clothes? Obviously there has to be more than that.

The point is, being an observant Jew, being a good person, involves more than the external observation. Clothes don't make the man.

Put Your Mask on First

On an airplane, Rabbi Feller was just dozing off when he heard that well-known litany the stewards go through each time.

"This cabin is pressurized for your comfort. If for any reason we lose cabin pressure, a row of oxygen masks will drop down in front of you. Pull your mask to you, put it over your nose and mouth, and breathe. Always be sure to put your own mask on first, before assisting any children."

But this time, when Rabbi Feller heard that message, he really *heard* it. "Did you get that?" he asked, sitting up.

"Get what?" I asked, having heard that message too many times to remember.

"What they said — about putting your own mask on first, and only then helping your children. Think about that," he said. "We spend all our time struggling to get the best for our children, before we think of ourselves. We give them the best food, so they'll grow and be healthy. If there's danger, we send them away and we stay to face it. We deny ourselves, so we can afford to give them the best education. It's a lifesaving thing — you might lose your life, but you save the child. But look at that a different way," he said. "I can raise all kinds of money for children's education, but what about an adult's need for learning, too. I think that's the message: Parents, put your masks on first!"

By all means, educate your children. But be sure that you, yourself, are involved in some learning, too. You can't help your child grow in Torah unless you are learning yourself. Before you put the mask on your child, be sure that your own mask is already in place.

THE GOAL OF FAILURE

The redemptive goal of failing is that you're less likely to make the same mistake again. But even if you really learned your lesson, and you don't repeat that error, there's obviously an infinite array of other mistakes still available.

It's sort of like Yom Kippur: You're confessing to God all the things you did wrong, in lush detail — not so much to reminisce, but rather to tell God how much you learned from it all. You learned what not to do, so the next time you're in that situation, you won't make that mistake again.

Perspective

A psychologist was treating a patient with serious problems. The patient was 22 years old and he wet his bed. He couldn't go out on a date. He couldn't go out with friends. He couldn't go camping. He was ashamed.

The shame was really persecuting him, and led to a deep, deep depression. My friend treated this man for many years, and finally he had success. I said, "What did you do? Is he no longer wetting his bed?"

"Oh, no," he said, "he wets his bed. But he's no longer ashamed."

Doing the proper thing is the channel for contentment and inner peace and G-d's blessings also in all personal affairs.

— *Rabbi Menachem Mendel Schneerson, 1978*

DIRTY WORK

A Russian fellow called Getzi Vilensky used to sit in the synagogue after praying and have a study session in Talmud. He said, "Don't worry, they know who I am. Just don't come too close to me because they will see that I'm associating with Americans and they'll come ask me for questioning."

Getzi worked in a big, government-owned department store. He worked for them for 20 years and he said he kept every Shabbos. How can you keep Shabbos? In Russia, Shabbos is a working day.

In this Russian store, the big problem was thievery, people would steal. So at night, when they closed the doors, they put dogs, dozens and dozens of dogs running through the store, to bite anyone sneaking anything. And these dogs, running loose, left their remnants behind, so someone had to go in the morning, every day, and clean up the dog mess in the whole store.

Getzi Vilensky volunteered to do this. He said to the person whose turn it was to clean up the dirt, "I'll clean up the dirt, you take my place for Shabbos." For 20 years, he never had to work on Shabbos. The *mesiras nefesh*, the self-sacrifice! Imagine, a Yid doing this filthy dirty job for the purpose of Shabbos.

TRAPPED

The KGB, like all police departments, knows that there are certain people breaking the law, but as long as they don't make waves about it, they leave them alone. So Getzi Vilensky said, "They know I *daven*, that I keep a *shiur* in Talmud, that everyone knows they can have a kosher meal at my house. But if they knew I was meeting Americans ..."

Something happened that was the most frightening moment in our life. Gail and I got to know Getzi Vilensky and we visited him often. We learned where he lived and how to take a subway there. He didn't ever want us to take a taxi to his place because the taxi drivers were in the employ of the KGB and would give them reports.

So we took the subway and walked to his place. When we got to his building, there was somebody in the elevator, a big Russian man. We got in the elevator and we were going to press the button, and the man said, "Which floor?" Now, to hear English spoken, we knew were trapped.

Gail thought quickly and gave him the wrong floor. Instead of saying three, she said four. He took us to four, and we walked down to one of the doors and she pressed the buzzer. I said, "What happens if someone is home?"

She said, "We can't allow them to find out that we're coming to visit Getzi, we can't."

Fortunately, no one was there.

So we came back to the elevator and she told the *goy*, "Down, please," and she said to me, "Uncle isn't home."

I was scared to death. We didn't take the subway. We walked

back and kept looking behind us to see if someone was following us. It must have been about four miles.

The profundity of monotheism, with which the Ten

Commandments begin, and the simplicity of the ethical and

moral laws, which the Ten Commandments conclude,

point to an important lesson, namely:

a) The true believer in G-d is not the one who holds abstract

ideas, but the one whose knowledge of G-d leads him to the

proper daily conduct even in ordinary and commonplace

matters, in his dealings with his neighbors and the respect for

their property, even if it be an ox or an ass, etc.

b) The ethical and moral laws, even those that are so obvious

as "Thou shalt not steal" and "Thou shalt not murder," will

have actual validity and will be observed only if they are based

on the first and second Commandments, that is to say, based

on Divine authority, the authority of the One and Only G-d.

— Rabbi Menachem Mendel Schneerson, 1964

SEE FOR YOURSELF

I n Al Capp's *Li'l Abner* cartoon, one segment had Li'l Abner become an astronaut. Some mad scientist had invented a space capsule, and they'd sent Li'l Abner to the moon, complete with a camera. He was supposed to take pictures of the moon, but instead he'd hooked up with a space creature who used up a whole roll of film taking pictures of him: Here's Li'l Abner eating a sandwich. Here's Li'l Abner tired and sitting down. Here's Li'l Abner drinking water — on and on. Each photo showed only Li'l Abner doing one thing or another — and nothing of the moon!

People still do that. They go on vacation and take pictures of themselves standing in front of every monument they run into — but all you can see is the person who's on vacation! In Israel, tourists stand in front of the Western Wall, the Kotel, and have someone take their picture. "Here's tourist so-and-so, in front of the Kotel." But what can you see of the Kotel?

Maybe it would be a good idea to put the camera away. Instead of focusing on the Kotel through the lens of the camera, go buy a postcard, if a picture is what you want.

While you're here, see the Kotel for yourself, with your own eyes. Try to absorb the holiness, the atmosphere, the timelessness. Don't block out the Kotel with pictures of yourself.

CHAPTER 2

DIVINE PROVIDENCE

There Are No Accidents

COINCIDENCE?

A lot of things happen in life that sound very, very coinciden-
tal. My first job was teaching in the first integrated college
in the United States, in Lafayette, LA, at a small college
called Southwestern Louisiana Institute. It was integrated by court
order. This was before the Civil Rights Movement was known as the
Civil Rights Movement, before Martin Luther King.

When the federal courts integrated it, half the faculty resigned,
so the president of the university was recruiting. Whom would they
recruit? Liberal Jews — they're the ones who were interested in it.
Without knowing that we were part of the Civil Rights Movement,
Gail — who was pregnant with our first little girl — and I took our
old car and drove down to Louisiana from Minnesota. I'll never forget that, going from the snow and ice to the azaleas blooming. And
I became a professor there.

Now, what's the coincidence? The following year there was a terrible outbreak of staphylococcus infections in the southern United
States. Before that, we were able to treat all these infections with penicillin, but this was the first appearance of penicillin-resistant staphy-
lococci bacteria that could not be controlled with the antibiotic.

I was the only bacteriologist in about a hundred square miles,
down in the swamps in Louisiana, so the medical profession asked
me to help them solve this issue. And we did. I didn't know what
we were doing, but we started instituting some practices, ordinary
sanitation, isolation, hand-washing. And it worked. So I wrote a
paper on this subject.

And believe it or not, within the next two years, that epidemic
had spread throughout the country — and Minnesota, being a big

university, got several million dollars to study this subject. They looked around for somebody to run the project and lo, they found me in this little jerkwater college. I was one of the few people who had written a paper on controlling an outbreak, so they brought us back to Minnesota. Coincidence?

A person, especially a Jew, and particularly one who has a

prominent position of influence in his surroundings,

should try to arrange his plans in a way that would produce

the maximum influence and benefit in one's surroundings;

with personal benefits and advantages being of secondary

consideration. Although in practice, we have seen that

Hatzlocho *(success) in the area of public good usually brings*

a greater measure of Hatzlocho *in one's personal affairs.*

—*Rabbi Menachem Mendel Schneerson, 1986*

INCREASED AWARENESS

A fundamental principle of *chassidus* emphasizes the role of divine providence in every event that occurs, regardless of the event's apparent insignificance. This principle, based on the mastery and eternal involvement of the Creator with His Creation, has an important corollary: Everything that is seen and heard is designed to increase a person's awareness of the Almighty and should teach a Jew how to fulfill the Almighty's instructions.

It follows that the everyday experiences and observations made even in the lecture room, the laboratory, the academic office, and the science conference room have a deeper meaning. These experiences must be analyzed not only for their obvious and external information, but also for the spiritual insights contained therein. In this fashion, they will provide the observer with a practical lesson in his continual attempt to discern and comply with the divine will as revealed in the Torah.

THE SOURCE

*A*t the first meeting I had with the Rebbe, I thought of a poem by Chaim Nachman Bialik. When I came into 770, the central headquarters of Chabad, on that Yud Tes Kislev, the 19th day of Kislev, a day of celebration chasidic circles the poem *"Oib Dyn Neshama Vill Dergayn Dem Kvall"* ("If Your Soul Wants to Get to the Bottom Source") by Bialik kept going through my mind, and I recited two or three of the verses.

I don't know if anyone ever recited Bialik to the Rebbe, but he said this is a sign of the *hashgochah protis* in everything. Everything that a Jew sees or hears is designed to bring him closer to God.

THE EPIDEMIC

I gnaz Semmelweis (1818-1865) was an assistant physician in the maternity unit of the Vienna General Hospital during the 1840s, when he stumbled on a momentous discovery — one that even he didn't fully understand.

In those days, puerperal "childbed" fever was a serious problem for both newborn babies and their mothers. At Vienna General, Semmelweis noticed something he couldn't explain: In the hospital's First Obstetrical Clinic, over 13 percent of the newborns died of the fever. But in the Second Obstetrical Clinic — in the same hospital — only 2 percent died. What could possibly cause the difference?

Understand, Semmelweis didn't have the faintest idea what caused the disease. This was 30 years before Louis Pasteur discovered that disease could be caused by microbes, long before Joseph Lister made public his ideas about sanitation and asepsis in operating rooms.

Semmelweis decided to try an experiment. He placed a big bowl of chlorine water — like household bleach — outside the delivery room, specifying that all doctors had to rinse their hands before entering the delivery room. Within two weeks, the mortality rate in the First Clinic, run by doctors, was equal to that of the Second, run by midwives.

That's the original medical story. But in terms of *hashgochah protis*, the story of Ignaz Semmelweis has other implications. Sometimes empirical knowledge — that which we gain by experience — can and should be used to stop an epidemic.

In our Jewish world, we can see that the incidence of Jewish dropouts, intermarriage, and assimilation is associated with certain activities. We can see and identify definite risk factors: the lack of Jewish education, the lack of Jewish summer camps, the lack of any protection against assimilation and loss of Jewish identity.

Even though we haven't perfected any psychological or socio-logical studies that would prove our thesis, we can see, based on simple observation, that there's a cause-and-effect factor involved in the loss of Jewish identity.

That's enough to employ empirical evidence — just like Sem-melweis did.

If you're worried about your grandchildren being Jewish, then you should worry about the Jewish education that their parents receive.

Our Sages say, "He who has 100, desires 200" — meaning

that ambition grows with achievement and even outpaces it.

And if this is so in material things,

how much more so in real and eternal values.

—Rabbi Menachem Mendel Schneerson, 1978

CHAPTER 3

SCIENCE AND RELIGION

There Are No Discrepancies

MAN ON THE MOON

In 1961, NASA became the big item on the agenda. In an address before a joint session of Congress, President Kennedy said that the American goal was to put a man on the moon within 10 years.

All of a sudden, billions of dollars were being appropriated to work in a field that no one knew anything about. I was a microbiologist who was looking for microbes on the walls of hospitals and bacteria in the air of laundries and operating rooms. So when NASA wanted to find out if there were any microbes in the stratosphere, believe it or not, I won the contract to explore the stratosphere for living micro-organisms.

That kicked off an entirely new world. I was really young — I must have been in my early 30s — and I got an unlimited amount of money to do research on things that no one had ever done before, so I became relatively famous.

DON'T PITY THE REBBE

The Rebbe asked if it would be possible to read some of the work I was doing for NASA, but only, as he pointed out very clearly, if it wasn't classified.

When the Rebbe first came to America, he was working at the Brooklyn Navy Yard and he had to have security clearance to work there, so he was very sensitive to this whole business of classified material. He used the word *classified*. He didn't use the word *secret*. Any type of classification, even confidential, he didn't want to know.

I said yeah, I think there are many documents I could send that are open, but I asked him, "Why should the Rebbe read this? Most of it is preliminary to going to Mars. We haven't been to Mars yet, we're just doing experiments to plan for the Martian trip. What we're doing is simply bacteriology, and that's not very exciting."

He said, "Let me decide, let me decide." So I promised him.

Several months went by and I didn't send him anything. The next time I was in New York, I was *davening Minchah* in 770, saying the afternoon prayers at Lubavitch headquarters, and the Rebbe saw me in the room. When *Minchah* was done, he called me over and he said, "You promised me something. Did you forget? You promised me the reports."

I made up an excuse. What should I say? "I was an idiot."

He said, "Don't say you're an idiot."

"Well, I thought the Rebbe has so much to do, he's so busy, why should he ..."

The Rebbe said something very important. He said, "Don't have pity on the Rebbe. Send the reports."

So I went home and I took a pile of reports, three of four folders full from different years of our work, and sent it to the Rebbe.

The discoveries in the natural sciences have thrown new light on the wonders of Creation, and the modern trend has consequently been towards the recognition of the unity pervading nature. In fact, with every advancement in science, the underlying unity in the physical world has become more clearly discernable; so much so, that science is now searching for the ideal formula which would comprise all the phenomena of the physical world in one comprehensive equation. With a little further insight it can be seen that the unity in Nature is the reflection of true monotheism in its Jewish concept. For as we Jews conceive of monotheism, is it not merely the belief that there is only One G-d, but that G-d's Unity transcends also the physical world, so that there is only one reality, namely G-d. However, inasmuch as Creation included all the souls, etc., there has been created a multiplicity and diversity in Nature — insofar as the created beings themselves are concerned, without, however, effecting any change in the Creator, as explained at length in Chassidus.

—Rabbi Menachem Mendel Schneerson, 1965

No Discrepancies

The first landing on Mars was July 1976. The work done in the late '60s and early '70s was trying to develop a device that would sample the dust on Mars and see if microbes are present. People like myself were in the job of seeing what type of microbes we might recognize if this was a Martian atmosphere, so we could provide the proper nutrients to grow them when we get there. That's what I did. It's a complicated thing, but it was basically simple bacteriology.

I had a big group of microbiologists working for me in the laboratory, testing and generating mounds and mounds and mounds of paper that we would send to NASA. Until we actually landed on Mars and took samples, nothing we were doing had any relevance to anything. However, I had these mounds and mounds of paper and documents, so I sent them to the Rebbe and he thanked me very much, as usual, with his modest approach, "I won't understand them, it's not my field, but I'm just interested in reading anyway."

The next audience Gail and I had with the Rebbe, we brought all our children. I remember one of the little girls was dancing on his table. Just before leaving, the Rebbe said, "There is something I'd like to bring up. Obviously, it's because I don't understand your work, but it seems to me there is a disagreement between something you wrote in one place about whether bacteria like these would grow on Mars" — and he mentioned a volume, this and this part of the report — "and in another report that you wrote several years later, you describe the same experiment and you say that they wouldn't grow on Mars."

So I said, "Well, I don't remember." By this time, you learned

60

that you don't ask him. You tell him, "I don't remember, but I'll look it up." When I came home, I found these dusty reports, I read them up, and of course there was a discrepancy. What I said here I didn't say here. Why not? Because I forgot what I said the first time. What difference did it make? It didn't make any essential difference and it was really a typographical mistake.

I came back to the Rebbe at the next *yechidus*, private audience, a year later. I said, "With regard to the discrepancy, the Rebbe was right. What I said here, I didn't say here. It was simply because I made a mistake and I hadn't read the first report when I wrote the second. I'm going to correct it."

He said, "Thank you. You make me feel better. I don't like contradictions in science." He used the word *stiros*, "I don't like discrepancies, contradictions. If the difference between what you said here and here is because you made a mistake, that makes me feel better."

The Rebbe kept looking for truth. A discrepancy like this is impossible unless it can be explained. You learn this from Gemarah. You learn this from basic Torah.

I have not the faintest idea why the Rebbe was interested in the scientific notes, but this was the nature of this particular person. Even in something as irrelevant as the growth of micro-organisms under certain conditions of pressure and temperature and nutrients — that there should be a report that says this and a report that says that — there's got to be some kind of reconciliation. And the reconciliation isn't a compromise, that they're both right. Uh uh. What was the reason for the discrepancy? There can be no discrepancies in a matter of truth.

THE COMPLEXITY OF SIMPLICITY

*N*ASA put together a team that was going to investigate space. As a PhD in microbiology, I was part of the team. There was a whole group of us. The plan was to send a satellite around the earth and let it orbit for maybe three days, 20 orbits or so, just like John Glenn. No humans would be aboard this spacecraft. Instead, it would be filled with scientific experiments of one sort or another, all designed to help us learn a little bit about what happens when you put live things into outer space and keep them there for a while.

We know that for all kinds of living things, when they are in their young, formative, sensitive stages, they're the most vulnerable. Most of the bad things that happen to children happen when they're the youngest — *in utero*, or relatively soon after birth. Plants are equally sensitive. So to get the greatest effect, we biologists decided to conduct our experiments on very young units — we had little worms, we had little sea urchins, and a few other young things. The idea was to put them in little containers, send them up, let them orbit for 20 revolutions, and then bring them down. Then we'd look to see what happened.

Another of the experiments we sent up involved the germination of seedlings — wheat, rye, and barley seeds, and green beans. This kind of experiment is a classic; everyone who's ever been to first grade has seen this: The teacher takes a bean seed, folds it into blotting paper or cotton batting, soaks it in water, and maybe puts it between two pieces of glass. Then you leave it alone for a little while, overnight, over Shabbat. When the kids come back to school, they're astonished: The seed has sprouted.

It's such a classic experiment, we know exactly how much time it takes any given seed to germinate. Understand, we have no idea at all what specifically triggers it, but we know the timeline. First, the seed coat will break, and a little sprig goes out from it, growing down. Almost inevitably, that first little sprig will be the root system, and it will grow down. Give it a bit more time, and that sprig will develop tiny root hairs, and it grows still more. In a couple of days, there's a pretty substantial root system.

An hour or two after the root breaks out, another string starts growing horizontally, and then it inevitably turns up. That's the stem. Within a day or two, it develops leaves, and then flowers. And there you have it: This little seed is now a bean plant.

This is the perfect example of the complexity of simplicity, and one of those everyday miracles that overwhelms me. Everything that plant needs to begin life is within the seed. All it needs is a little water and a bit of nurture.

So at NASA, we sent up our seedlings, and we brought them back. When we opened the container, there wasn't a single person in the room who wasn't completely fascinated. Unbelievable!

The seedlings had germinated. They sprouted, just as they would have on earth. Indeed, the root sprig began growing downward. But then, chaos intervened. Instead of continuing down, the roots radically bent sideways, or horizontally. Sometimes they started growing up, sometimes they turned back and grew down again, in a loop. Understand: It was a root. It had the requisite root hairs. But the system didn't grow in any predictable fashion, it just meandered around in chaos. It was a freak of nature, or to use a very scientific term, a monster.

The same was true of the stem: It sprouted just fine, but from there, all was chaos. The stem didn't grow up, it jutted here and there, back and forth, in loops and whirls. Unlike anything I'd ever seen.

I took the pictures of our seedlings and brought them to the Lubavitcher Rebbe. He gazed at them, as fascinated as I was. "See?" he said. "Even a plant needs to know what's up and what's down. Even a plant knows where up is."

Today we know a little more about it. Hormones are involved in determining the direction in which the germinating shoots will grow. In fact, we know now that you can correct the damage. Put the seedling into a centrifuge, and restore the elements of gravity that had been withheld. Given some sense of gravity, the seedling corrects itself, and will grow up and down.

But everything — even a simple plant — needs to have an orientation.

Clearly, one who has the qualification to influence others is not to consider himself an ordinary draftee, but rather a Commanding Officer in G-d's Army, and one who has even greater qualifications to lead and inspire such "Officers" should consider himself a General.

— Rabbi Menachem Mendel Schneerson, 1974

PERSPECTIVE

W hen you're on earth, it's difficult to get a good perspective of what it's like on the moon.

Well, if you're going to safely land a space vehicle on the moon, you need accurate information about how high the outcroppings are so you can avoid them, and how deep the craters are, to see what kind of obstacle they actually present. So we sent up Lunar Orbiter.

With two sets of photos, taken of the same places we'd previously mapped, we were able to mathematically calculate how high the outcroppings were, and how deep the craters. Two sets, taken from different perspectives, allowed a three-dimensional map to be constructed. Without that, the human flight to the moon, the Apollo landing, would have been too risky to undertake.

In our society, we always have conflicting forces acting on us. There's the material and the spiritual, outcroppings and craters, each pulling in its own direction. When you look at the panoply of religious alternatives — Orthodox, Reform, Conservative, Reconstructionist, and all the rest — it's very difficult to thread your way through.

You need to get an additional perspective.

When the chasidic movement began, it was much maligned. "They pervert Torah," was the complaint. In response, the chasidic rebbes said, "We haven't perverted Torah. We're just giving you a different perspective on Torah you haven't heard before."

Without two viewpoints, you can't gain perspective. You'll never get a real picture of anything without seeing it from at least two directions.

LIFE ON MARS

When people asked Rabbi Feller what I do, he told them, "He works for NASA and he is looking for life on Mars." Other *Chasidim* said, "You mustn't — *assur* — it's forbidden."

So Rabbi Feller said to me, "There are those people who think you shouldn't be doing this kind of work. Why don't you ask the Rebbe?"

I did. While we were talking, I said, "You know, there are those of your followers who say that a Jew should not be working in the Space Biology program, because it goes contrary to Torah."

The Rebbe stopped — one of those beautiful moments in time — he didn't smile, he just thought, and then he pointed at me and he said in Yiddish, "You should look for life on Mars and you should keep looking. And if you don't find it, keep looking elsewhere and elsewhere, because to sit here in this world and say there is no life elsewhere is to put a limit around what God can do — and *that* nobody can do."

JEWISH EDUCATION AND SPACE FLIGHT

The Rebbe, who was trained as an engineer, had a keen understanding of the physical world and how it worked. So when the Apollo spaceship landed on the moon in 1969, he used that scientific achievement to make a point about Jewish education.

In the NASA program, the Rebbe understood, there had always been a problem with balancing weight limits versus fuel needs in space flights. It's a conundrum: If you build a rocket that will go a long distance, you'll need to carry a lot of fuel. But the more fuel you carry, the larger the fuel container has to be — which means the weight of the spacecraft is increased. The heavier the spacecraft, the more fuel you need. It's an endless cycle, and a critical issue if your mission takes you beyond the local environment to the moon or Mars.

Engineers settled on a solution: They built multi-staged rockets that contain several individual fuel tanks. The largest amount of fuel is needed in the first minutes of the flight, as the rocket takes off from the ground. So the fuel for those first four or five minutes goes into a separate container, and when the fuel is used, the empty container is jettisoned off. When you watch a launch, you'll see it. After a few minutes, the used-up fuel container drops away.

The next stage of the flight uses up the next-most fuel, because the rocket is still fighting the gravity of the earth. When that fuel tank is empty, it's also jettisoned, as are several more stages. As each tank of fuel is used and the container jettisoned, the overall weight of the spacecraft becomes lighter, so it needs less fuel.

By the time you're weightless, out of the pull of the earth's gravity, you'll need only a tiny bit of fuel. Because there's no resistance to fight against, a thimbleful of fuel will propel the craft a very long distance.

So the Rebbe used this to explain a passage in Mishle (Proverbs 22:6), where it's brought down that we are to "Educate a young person according to his path." That phrase has always been problematical, the Rebbe said. What does it mean, "according to his path"? It's very simple, the Rebbe said. It's something we do in education all the time. We introduce a three-year-old child to the *aleph-bet*, and we make a big fuss about it. We have a party, we give him candy, we celebrate. In the old days, we'd even put honey on the page itself. The child sees the big fuss, he likes the candy, and he's very interested. He learns.

When the child gets to be about five years old, candy doesn't motivate him anymore. So we move to a different incentive, maybe toys or a tricycle.

Then when he's 10 or 11, toys don't work anymore. By that time, he wants electronic games. That's what we're doing — educating a child according to his path. We're using an incentive that's meaningful to him at his age level.

When he gets to be 18 or 19, things really change. He's surely no longer interested in honey on the page, or toys, or even electronic games. By that time, we might remind him that the brightest students get the prettiest wives — Jewish eugenics!

This, the Rebbe said, is exactly the same principle as that of the multi-stage rocket. That which is not needed any longer is jettisoned. We don't want to carry the extra weight along.

When you reach the next level of understanding and learning, you get rid of the weight, you don't need as much inspiration as before in order to push yourself. By the time you reach a certain stage of learning, all you need is just a tiny bit of fuel to propel you forward.

If in a previous generation there were people who doubted the

need of Divine authority for common morality and ethics,

in the belief that human reason is sufficient authority

for morality and ethics, our present generation has,

unfortunately, in a most devastating and tragic way, refuted

this mistaken notion. For, it is precisely the nation which had

excelled itself in the exact sciences, the humanities and even in

philosophy and ethics, that turned out to be the most depraved

nation of the world, making an ideal of murder and robbery,

etc. Anyone who knows how insignificant was the minority

of Germans who opposed the Hitler regime realizes that the

German cult was not something which was practiced by a few

individuals, but had embraced the vast majority of that nation,

who considered itself a "super race," etc.

—*Rabbi Menachem Mendel Schneerson, 1964*

THE MEANING OF LIFE

I n 1961, President Kennedy firmly committed the U.S. to landing a man on the moon by the end of the decade. You know what that means. When the commander-in-chief says, "Jump!" we at NASA didn't even have to ask, "How high?" We already knew: as high as the moon.

It was audacious, when you think about it. The president announced his national goal, and we were obliged to pull it off, ready or not. At this point, we hadn't even seen the back side of the moon! The truth is, we weren't even completely sure it wasn't made of green cheese! Or, as one of our professors asked, "What if the moon is made of Jell-O powder? What if our spacecraft landed on the moon, and then returned, splashed down in the sea, and the whole ocean coagulated?! We just didn't have any idea.

I was part of the team of biologists — although I use that word advisedly. What in heck is a *biologist*? You can be a zoologist and know something about animals, or you can be a botanist and know something about plants. But what's a biologist? So far as I know, a biologist is a high school teacher — that's the only place they exist. How could anyone study *life*? We can't even define it!

How do you define life? What would the elements be?

Let's say we go up to Mars and we're going to search for life. The first thing we'd do is search for things we know are alive when we see them here on earth.

We'd look for things we know — plants, animals, microbes, that sort of thing.

But why would we be so arrogant as to assume that life cycles on Mars are the same as we have here on earth? If we go to Mars and expect to find a field of wildflowers, and we actually see wild-flowers, then fine. There's life. But if we don't see wildflowers, then there's no life?

In winter, during my classes in Minneapolis, I have my students look out the window and I direct their attention to a little group of oak trees standing in maybe two to three feet of snow.

I ask them: "Suppose I told you that of those six trees, two are dead and four are living. How would you decide which ones are alive?"

The truth is, with those trees, you can't tell which ones are alive until spring comes.

The definition of life is not an absolute thing. It depends on opportunity. A thing can be alive but in a dormant state, and you can't tell until you give the thing an opportunity to flourish.

The Rebbe was famous for never, ever, accepting a pessimistic point of view. He always insisted on assuming the best, the most optimistic scenario. In all of his outreach work to Jews all over the world, he always assumed that every Jew would happily adopt a Torah way of life if he just had the opportunity.

You have to give Torah an opportunity. When you give a Jew an opportunity to come closer to God, he'll take that opportunity, and he'll love it. He will flourish. You might have to wait until spring-time, of course. Life is there, but you can't see it all the time.

And what if you can't wait until springtime? Then you'd better make some artificial springtime right now. Bring springtime into the world, right now. Whatever the season.

IF ALL ELSE FAILS

The team at NASA bought an expensive instrument for a research project. I'd like to say it was a computer, but in all honesty, it wasn't quite that. It was an analytical device of some now-primitive sort, but at the time, it seemed exquisitely complicated.

The intelligent and perceptive people who packaged that piece of equipment sent with it a rather sizeable booklet with directions for proper assembly and use. The handbook was well indexed, and probably comprehensible if you settled down to study it. They also enclosed a poster, saying that after the unit was properly assembled, the poster should be hung on the wall in reasonable proximity to the equipment.

The poster contained one simple sentence:

"If all else fails, read the directions."

It's similar to a chasidic saying:

"Things are so desperate, we can't depend on miracles anymore. It's time to say *Tehillim*, Psalms."

FROM GENERATION TO GENERATION

I n the 1960s and '70s, those working in the NASA program were preparing to launch the first rocket that would land on the planet Mars. In 1976, we landed two manmade objects on Mars — Vikings I and II. Never before in history had mankind penetrated that far into space. I was one of the principal investigators on the Viking program, having designed two major research projects.

The timing of these programs in unique: We were the microbiologists, and we were required to have our projects designed and ready six or seven years before launch. The engineers needed adequate time to design the spacecraft to hold it all. So several years before launch, we had essentially finished our work. But since we were still getting paid by NASA, they felt compelled to find something useful for us to do.

One of the program managers called a meeting for the 30 or so of us involved. He began talking about the real challenges of space flight, predicting that after we explored our own solar system, we'd move into interstellar space — go to the stars. This was the topic we were to explore.

The nearest star is Alpha Centauri. It's 4.1 light years away from earth, which means that a beam of light traveling at a speed of 186,000 miles per second would take 4.1 years to reach Alpha Centauri.

Needless to say, we were a long way from traveling at that speed. I did the calculations, and even if we managed to build a rocket that would travel 100 times faster than anything we'd ever designed, it would still take 830 years to get there and another 830 to come home again, of course!

As someone said, "No more coffee breaks — we'd better get going!"

Obviously, sending an astronaut wouldn't work, no one could live that long. There have been movies made about suspended animation — putting humans into some kind of deep sleep, where they don't age — but we don't know much about that. What we do know is that humans live 60-80 years, and then we die.

The only real solution is to put men and women together on a spaceship, and then advise them to follow the first commandment: Be fruitful and multiply. They would have children, who would marry other children, on and on and on, for many generations.

But it doesn't take a rocket scientist to see that this plan presents sociological problems, as well as an engineering issue. How would successive generations of people survive for the 830 years out, and the 830 years back?

Food is an obvious problem: What will they eat? Remember, there is nothing *out there*. Absolutely every scrap of everything they will need to live must be taken along or grown. There are no resources in space. Nothing.

Pondering this problem occupied a lot of NASA time. One possible solution is the extensive use of algae. There's sunlight in most of outer space, so algae could be grown on the collected sweat and urine from the humans. But people don't like to eat algae. Russian scientists at one time considered feeding the algae to chickens, and then the people could eat the chickens. But that leaves you with a feather problem. Feathers can't be recycled. What can you do with the feathers?

Of course it didn't take long to realize that the problems of space travel are almost the same as the problems of planet earth: Feeding a growing world population, supplying clean water, dealing with wastes of all kinds. This NASA project had many useful applications.

Waste was a big issue. What to do with it? Throw it out, or jettison it, like the spent fuel containers? But one of Newton's theories is that if you throw something out of a capsule traveling that fast, it will just go along with you. You can't get rid of it — but neither can you afford to waste it, whatever it is.

Other problems abound: If a group of people are confined together for 830 years, how can you make them get along? The history of mankind tells you that there's never been a 40-year period without one group of people deciding to eliminate another. In Jewish history, 40 years of peace is a very long time indeed.

I'm told there's a story in the Talmud about two people in a boat. One says, "I don't like you, so I'm going to drill a hole in your end of the boat." Just like a spaceship — you can't blow up just one end. Leisure is another issue: What will the people do? Once the space ship is en route, only a few minutes a day will be required to run it. What will everyone do with all that leisure? Unless we can design projects to successfully occupy time, problems will result.

As our seminar progressed, we discussed all these issues. Then another one popped up that fascinated me: How would the adults teach their children about themselves and their mission?

Think about it: For 830 years, all they have is the one instruction manual they started out with. But we know how we feel about old instructions — if an appliance handbook were written in Elizabethan English, we'd ignore it. Junk it! It's too old to be practical. Even maps — we don't follow old maps, we correct them!

But here's this spaceship full of people. If they junk the old instruction manual, what will happen? If they start fiddling around, tinkering with the maps and the navigational system, one thing is guaranteed: They'll get lost. And then how will they land the thing? And get back? Would that happen?

Well, we Americans are enamored with the vote. Who can doubt that a popular vote would override whatever advice the scientists and engineers were offering?

At the NASA meeting, the professor then made an interesting suggestion. "There are very few precedents for this kind of situation," he said. "How does a society pass down its mission and beliefs to succeeding generations? I think we need to study the Jewish system. So far as I know, they're the only group of people who, for thousands of years, have managed to hand down their traditions intact to each new generation. We should study the Jews, and see how they did it."

Now that was interesting, more than enough to set my own mind to work, long after the session ended. I came to some additional considerations myself.

As Jews, we do indeed have a continuous debate going on. Every day, wherever there are Jews, they still debate and discuss what exactly Moshe Rebbenu heard from God, what Moses heard from God, and how that applies to the problems we face this afternoon.

For several thousand years, our concept of our mission has remained real. It's not a hypothetical. You can't study the Talmud without gaining the sense of the continuity. I can look and see what was added. I may know that this did — or that did not — come down from Sinai, but the message we received at Sinai is undiluted. It's as clear and precise today as it was when the Torah was given. The people who are guiding Jewish destiny know exactly what they're doing. They're successfully transmitting it to their children.

But the truth is, there's a bigger problem for multi-generational space travel than just retaining a sense of mission. The real problem is that after the first two hours, after the ship leaves the gravitational pull of the earth, from that moment on, everyone, for all generations, will live in a weightless environment. Don't get me wrong, I love weightlessness. Leaping from place to place, dropping things that don't fall. It's great.

The point is, for 830 years, they all will live in a world with no gravity. The very memory of gravity will become so distant it won't be more than a legend, something that existed far in the past. But assigning the concept of gravity to the ancient bin of legends — along with trolls and angels and talking snakes — means that when they need to deal with it again, when 830 years later they come within the gravitational pull of Alpha Centauri, they won't have the vaguest notion of what gravity is, or how it works.

It's not even something as basic as figuring out how to land the ship. It's more fundamental: In a weightless environment, there is no up or down or front or back. There is no direction. So how do you know how to orient the spaceship when you want to land? And if you tore up that part of the instruction manual 800 years ago, you've got a problem. Even if you saved the manual, you have to learn — from scratch — what gravity is.

How can you teach the concept of gravity? It's different than transmitting a common mission. It's much harder; you have to transmit a concept that's not real, something that no one present ever experienced. The concept of reality that the spaceship people lived with for 830 years is not the model they can live with once they land.

So I thought about it. If I were a principal investigator on that mission, I'd do it this way: I'd choose one man in the entire group.

Make it a trustworthy guy, maybe someone who's a little naïve, but someone I could trust.

Then I'd say to him, "Abe?" — and yes, I'd call him Abe — I'd say, "Abe? In addition to all that other stuff you're worrying about — where the food will come from, how to get rid of waste, how to keep wars from breaking out — there's something else you have to consider. You have to learn which way is up."

I'd tell him, "Abe, learn which way is up, which way is down. Learn the difference between transient and permanent. Learn to distinguish between ephemeral and real. And Abe, you have to teach that to your children, and have them teach it to their children, and on and on and on. Because if you miss even one generation, you're all lost. It will all disappear. People will not like the message, they will ridicule you, beat you, shoot you, gas you. But you must do it, or the whole mission was a waste."

When you think about it, the fact that we're all here talking about this is pretty good evidence that when Someone tried this experiment once before, it must have worked. Not perfectly, of course. But well enough.

CHAPTER 4

RELIGION AND SCIENCE

We Don't Know Anything

IT IS NOT MY JOB TO WIN ARGUMENTS

The Rebbe had written a famous letter on evolution. It wasn't to me, it was to somebody else whom I don't know. But that letter became a sort of pocket guidebook for any *shaliach*, any emissary, who was asked a question about science and religion.

I had already met the Rebbe, we were already close. So during a discussion, Moshe Feller pulled out the letter and had me read it. I had a negative approach to it. I thought it wasn't adequate. It was too thin. It was too threadbare. It wouldn't stand up in the argument of science. And I told that to Moshe. I said it's not a great letter. To say to Moshe Feller that a letter of the Rebbe's is not a great letter … So he said, "Why don't you write the Rebbe and tell him that?"

I said, "I'm not going to write to the Rebbe. I saw the Rebbe. I consider him to be the *navi* of our people. Before anything else, he is a *navi*, a prophet. I'm going to write him?"

"He'd like to hear from you." So I wrote the Rebbe a letter. I typed it out. I said, "My dear Rabbi Schneerson …" You know, after all, the Rebbe is the Rebbe, but that's the way you write a letter.

I wrote, "Dear Rabbi Schneerson, I saw this and this and I have the following criticism to make about it or comments to make about it … One, two, three, four … So as you will see from these particular …"

The Rebbe answered, first of all, about my appearance at the *farbrengen*, the gathering where we first met, and about a talk I gave on my impression of the *farbrengen*. He wrote another letter about another subject, but he never returned to the questions that I wrote in this particular letter.

So I wrote back, and he said I'm very happy to get all these letters from you — and every two months or so I would get a letter. So I said but you didn't answer the original questions, which means obviously that you agree with my point of view. I wrote the Rebbe criticizing, actually, literally criticizing, what he said in this letter about evolution and he didn't answer. He answered about another thing and another thing.

Finally, there is one letter in which the Rebbe says essentially that he has received regards from me from the *shluchim*, the Chabad emissaries, who came for the summer, and he knows now that we're sending our children to Gan Yisrael Day Camp, and this means that my wife is going along with my outlook in getting closer and closer to *Yiddishkeit*. So he will now go back to something I raised earlier but he did not want to touch because of the delicacy of the situation, because, as the Rebbe says, "It is not my job to win arguments. My job is to present the Jewish point of view and win adherence to the Jewish cause, and if I were to take issue with you on that letter, I might have pushed you away. But now that I see that you and your wife are — I will return ..." And he goes ahead and answers the letter with a reasonable explanation.

THERE IS ONLY ONE TRUTH

*N*ow, whether it convinced me or not, I don't know, but I saw something extremely important in that letter. The Rebbe doesn't argue about evolution or lack of. The Rebbe is demanding from scientists to teach science properly. In other words, to keep science from becoming a dogma. Science is a subject that must deal with probabilities rather than absolutes. Science deals with a hypothesis that must be developed and analyzed and tested and analyzed and refined and tested, and so on. That's what science is.

If we try and shortcut it and present a simple, straightforward picture — like most of the people are trying to do with evolution — it isn't a question of teaching right or wrong, it's a question that you're not being honest. And this is what the Rebbe continually insists on.

Some of the *Chasidim* even say they want Professor Greene to speak and to knock science. I don't knock science. What we knock is the insincerity, if you will; scientists who say things when they should be saying *I don't know*. The same thing with people who teach Torah who should sometimes say *I don't know*, or that there are several opinions, and that though the *Halachah*, the law, comes down in this, there still is — even in the Supreme Court — a majority and a minority opinion.

These are things that are part of our rational beings, our rational understanding of anything. So this attracted me very, very much to him because the Rebbe simply said, in one of the letters, that when he studied mathematics in Berlin and engineering in Paris, his only desire in his debates and discussions with other scientists was to be honest, to present a point of view.

We're always trying to get closer to the truth. But there is only one truth, the Rebbe says, only one truth — and that's the truth that is taught in the Torah. So therefore, if you're going to have a test of the validity of science with Torah, you must know what you're talking about.

I send you my prayerful wishes to utilize all your capacities in

a way that will give you complete personal satisfaction,

as well as bring satisfaction to all who benefit from your

good influence, and may all this be in the fullest measure of

Simcha (joy), in accordance with the saying of our Sages that

"Simcha breaks through barriers."

— *Rabbi Menachem Mendel Schneerson, 1976*

A Sense of Purpose

What is the purpose of all of this? How can you ask what is the purpose of a Jew without asking what is the purpose of creation in the first place? What is the purpose of that dog that was barking? What is the purpose of the plants that are growing? What is the purpose?

Yiddishkeit and the Torah tell us the purpose. The Rebbe was able to provide a coherence in all of these deep questions, and it makes sense. To a scientist, that's the most important thing in the world: coherence. Does it make sense, does it fit, does it interdigitate, does it stand?

GREEN DINOSAURS

When I was a very young graduate student, whenever I was in New York, I'd gravitate to the Museum of Natural History. I've always been fascinated with the diversity of human life, including the theory of evolution.

I never missed the dinosaur exhibits. Every time I went, I saw something new and interesting. Eventually the curators came to know me, and they'd allow me into the back-room workshops where the structures were being fashioned. That was the most fascinating of all.

Everyone knows what the dinosaurs looked like, right? Everyone's seen either the incredible displays here, or at the Smithsonian in Washington, or smaller museums. When I was in the back room at the museum, watching them reconstruct one of the huge skeletons, I thought that was the essence of pure science.

Very rarely, of course, was the entire skeleton of a dinosaur found. For the most part, what the technicians did was to piece together a skeleton, using what they'd found in several different places. Some of the bones were real, ossified bones from one site or another, and others were artificial, reconstructed bones made to replace those that were not available. These were made — in those days — of plaster of Paris.

The genius of the workers is that they were able to interpolate the parts that were missing, working with the bones they had. If they knew an animal had five vertebrae, but they had only three actual bones, they'd be able to reconstruct what the other two would look like.

Now understand, this was in the 1950s, long before I ever ran across Rabbi Feller or the Rebbe. It was long before I began piecing the elements of Judaism together in my mind. In retrospect, I believe I was potentiated, even then. My soul was cast in a Jewish mold, with only a hint of where I would ultimately find myself once I began a spiritual journey, in addition to delving into the secrets of science.

Maybe the most fascinating part of it all was what today we take for granted as forensic science — first reconstructing the framework, the skeleton, then putting the musculature over it. They could tell from the way the bones grew, and how they were positioned within the body, what kind of muscular structure they supported. This takes a tremendous amount of knowledge and skill, to reconstruct how big the muscles were, how the tendons lay. They'd extrapolate from the size of one known body part — like the feet — how big the haunches were, or where the spine curved. When that was done, they'd even re-create the head, based on the skull structure.

The finishing touches came when they re-created skin, and produced an animal that — they said — looked like those that had actually wandered the earth. But this part wasn't based exactly on knowledge, because of course no one has ever seen dinosaur flesh. We've seen mammoths — we've found them reasonably intact — but they weren't of the same vintage. For the dinosaurs, it was pure speculation. Even so, when they finished, they'd take the photographs and put them in textbooks. This, they said, is what a dinosaur looked like.

You know the pictures — the skin of a dinosaur is greenish, maybe with a muddy blue tinge. It had little stipples in it, little dimples. Way before Spielberg, way before Crichton and *Jurassic Park*, we all knew exactly what a dinosaur looked like — we'd seen the pictures in our grade-school textbooks. Obviously, we'd know a dinosaur when we saw it!

My problem was, I was a grad student. I was on a search for truth as well as life. Everything had to be consistent.

So I asked the man who was there working with it, "Why is that dinosaur green?"

And he looked at me a little strange, but said, "Because dinosaurs are green."

Then he thought about it for a moment, and asked, "Why? What color do you think they should be?"

Believe it or not, this is a conversation that came to figure hugely in my life. It was a prime moment.

So I thought about his question. Then I said, "Well, I don't really know. How about pink? Or they could be blue or have yellow polka dots." Now this was way before the Flintstones, too — maybe they got the idea from me.

The technician became very offended. "That's ridiculous," he said. "Who ever saw a yellow dinosaur?"

To which I obviously responded, "Who ever saw a green one?"

In terms of teachable moments, that was a big one. It taught me one of life's most valuable lessons.

I learned that science in itself contains a lot of speculation and extrapolation. A good scientist is one who uses those tools, but he knows and acknowledges the difference between what he *knows* and when he's merely speculating.

That's truth. It's good to know.

THE ANSWER

One of the great things that I continually discover in my work is how much we don't know. Everything that is being discovered today or tomorrow will uncover not areas of new knowledge, but areas of past ignorance. We're going to find out tomorrow that the things we thought we knew today, we didn't really know.

Take a look at the Hubble telescope. Every day this Hubble telescope comes back with new pictures from farther and farther away. Before they launched the Hubble telescope, there were pretty good books describing what the universe was like. And overnight, it's different.

Did the universe change because they went ahead with a telescope? No — we were wrong. Those books that were published were wrong. The Copernican theory of the solar system and the Ptolemaic theory? *Shtuyot*, nonsense. Listen, it's fine, it's a good argument, but don't bet your life on it and don't bet your children's life on it.

This is the answer. That's what I learned — not from the Rebbe, but in studying the Torah of the Rebbe, and studying Tanya, and studying Rashi.

The relationship with the Rebbe was simply a backing away a bit, because the light is very strong, much stronger than I ever anticipated, to learn just a little bit and then realize how little I knew. I got to speak to a person like the Rebbe, who had the tolerance to sit in a room with me wearing a stupid hat or arguing a certain point. I feel a little embarrassed, like a child does sometimes when the parents bring up something he drew in kindergarten.

We all progress, I hope. The most important thing is the awareness; I'm talking about the whole world of Torah, the whole field of science, the development of a human being.

I'm very jealous of the time because I'm getting older and I realize that in the reality of things, I'm not going to have enough time to get the answers to all these questions, because every time we answer something, we learn there is so much more to be learned. We don't know anything.

May G-d grant that all matters should be in accordance with the words of the Megillah, "For the Jews there was light, joy, gladness and honor." May this be fulfilled also in the case of each and every one of us...in accordance with the traditional text which we add to this quotation..., "So it be for us," at the termination of Shabbos and Yom Tov (holy days), when going back to the ordinary days of the week, and it is necessary to make Chol *(secular) into* Kodesh *(holy).*

— *Rabbi Menachem Mendel Schneerson, 1968*

THE MIRACLE OF BIRTH

O ne of the most amazing things — if we had to describe it in any word in the English language, it would be a *miracle* — happens every time a living creature is born. Every creature that at least has a backbone, and in whom fertilization is from a male and a female, has a process in which the fetus, formed by the joining of the two cells from the father and from the mother, becomes many cells, which develop into a fetus or an embryo.

For several months, depending on the creature — in mice, it's just a couple of weeks; in sheep, it's a couple of months; in horses, a year or so; the human being is nine months — that creature is what we call *aquatic*, it lives surrounded by water completely. If that fetus is taken out, it will die immediately. It's surrounded by water. It doesn't breathe. It doesn't eat. It gets all its nutrients through the umbilical cord.

And suddenly, the mother comes into the hospital to have a baby and within minutes — not hours — that fetus changes from a completely aquatic creature to completely dry. Two minutes after that baby is born, if you put it back into the uterus, it will drown. It's now become an air-breathing creature. Two minutes before it was born, if it started to breathe, it would drown.

For many years, we talked about the miracle of birth — but it was nonsense, because we didn't know the miracle of it. In the mother's uterus, we have lungs but they are flat, and in order to breathe, they have to expand. If they expanded two minutes before, the baby would drown. If they don't expand, it will die of suffocation.

We're breathing right now. We breathe in the air and it goes through our lungs. From the other side, blood comes and the air meets the blood and the oxygen is transferred into carbon dioxide. Everyone understands this. OK, fantastic. But when we're in the mother's uterus, we're not breathing, so the blood doesn't have to go through the lungs. There is actually a duct. Instead of going from the heart to the lungs and then back into the blood system, it goes directly from the heart into the circulatory system because we have a tube that feeds it.

If this tube stays open after you're born, you won't breathe again, even if the lungs are expanded, because all the blood is being drained back. This is what's called *patent ductus arteriosus.* It has to close off. There is a hole between the top two chambers of the heart, the left and the right, that has to heal within a short period of time. If it doesn't, it becomes a blue baby.

We're learning, we're learning, we're learning.

The point I'm making is that we didn't know about all this. All we knew is that a baby is born. We're just beginning to learn the hundreds of things that have to happen to make it work. There is nothing more complicated. Dozens and dozens and dozens of different hormones and enzymes have to occur without anyone directing. It's an amazing thing.

Literal or Figurative?

The textbook they used in our Sunday school in Lafayette, LA, explained that we really have to consider the Torah as allegory and analogy rather than literally, because there is an immediate discrepancy between the story of creation.

In one place it talks about creating man on the sixth day, and in the other place it talks about how God took the mud from the earth and raised life. There are two separate stories, so therefore none of them are true.

The person who wrote this never read Rashi.

UNIVERSAL QUESTIONS

Various *shluchim* centers were being created around the world, and I was invited relatively frequently to speak at the openings. It was not too bad when there were a couple of dozen.

When they became a couple of hundred and into the thousands, it put a certain stress on me. I don't think I was anywhere near all of them, but I have a journal and I counted them up. I have probably spoken at between 700 and 900 different *shluchim* centers.

When they're opening up the campuses, I go to them. I enjoy meeting college students and college professors. Quite frankly, it's not a question of bragging, but there are very few questions that the kids have nowadays that are really new. Nothing really happened in science or the world that has changed the questions.

It was the same questions I used to ask myself before I met Rabbi Feller — these problems of science and religion, the problem of God, the problem of good and evil, the problem of coherence in life, the problem of life and death, the problem of ethics. All these various things are universal.

People have questions, and I have a rapport. I don't know if I have the answers but I can talk to kids. Give kids an opportunity, and they will search. They have to find some meaning. They're looking for meaning.

TORAH AND TIME ZONES

The Rebbe used modern concepts like time zones to illuminate Torah concepts.

In the Torah, he would say, we are given very specific instructions about the timing of Jewish holidays. When dealing with Passover, the Torah tells us specifically that on the 10th of the Jewish month Nissan, you are to buy your sheep. You keep it until the 15th of Nissan, and that's Pesach. So we all know: When the 15th of Nissan arrives, it's Passover, wherever you happen to be. When it's the 15th in Jerusalem or Beersheva, Pesach arrives there — even though in Minneapolis, it's still daylight. Pesach comes to Minneapolis when the sun sets there. It's always the 15th of Nissan.

The same is true of Sukkot, which is celebrated on the 15th day of the month of Tishrei. The Torah gives us the date.

But the third of the *regalim*, the pilgrim holidays, is different. For Shavuot, the Torah doesn't give us any date. We know it will fall on the sixth of Sivan. We can do the calculations. The Torah says that on the day after Pesach you count 49 days, and on the 50th, you bring the offerings. That's Shavuot. But it doesn't give the date.

Isn't that interesting? The Torah sets forth a specific date for Pesach and Sukkot, but not for Shavuot.

There are no accidents in Torah, no literary tricks. Every word that appears there, every letter — even every space between every letter — is meaningful. It tells us something. So if a specific date is given for two of the *regalim* but not for the third, there must be a reason.

The problem becomes more interesting with the advent of air travel. Suppose you're flying from San Francisco to Australia. On that trip, you pass over the time marker known as the International Date Line. If you happen to be traveling during the days between Pesach and Shavuot, you're counting days. But when you pass over the International Date Line, you either lose a day or gain it, depending on which direction you're flying. Your count will be different from the people in the place where you arrive — you'll lose a day or gain a day — while their count is straightforward.

Is that what the Torah intends? That you could be in the same city, but celebrate Shavuot on a different date than the local Jews? Now remember, this is Shavuot — it's a one-day holiday. It has nothing at all to do with being in *galut*, in the diaspora, where some holidays are celebrated for two days.

The answer, the Rebbe said, is relatively easy. The essence of Shavuot is more than just the festival of the first fruits, or of an agricultural holiday. Shavuot is also *Matan Torah*, the day the Torah was given to us on Sinai.

So is it not possible, the Rebbe asks, that God is telling us something about our own progress toward Torah? Shavuot celebrates the time when the Torah was given to each of us, individually and for all time. But perhaps the message of the missing date is that each of us comes to the Torah at our own pace — some a little earlier, some a little later.

When it comes to accepting the Torah, some come a little faster, some a little slower, each in his own time.

THE NATURAL CYCLE OF *TZEDAKAH*

Rabbi Hodakov was the Rebbe's personal secretary. He was the closest person in the world to the Rebbe. They'd known each other since they were young men, since both were in Riga in the 1920s.

A warm and personable man, Rabbi Hodakov would frequently tease me, "You're a scientist?" he'd say. "Let me teach you some science."

One day he said, "Do you know about the natural cycles of the elements?"

Well, I had some idea.

He recounted the process: "You know the carbon cycle: The human being or the animal eats food with carbon in it, and in the process of digestion, the animal oxidizes it, creating carbon dioxide, which he breathes out. Plants absorb the carbon dioxide and turn it into plant protoplasm — carbohydrates or starch. Then the man or the animal eats the plant — and maybe he's getting his own carbon back. It's possible! The cycle keeps repeating, going round and round, coming back over and over again."

Then he asked, "What would you do if either the plant or the animal decided to stop? What if the cow who eats the grass says, 'No, that's it! I'm not going to breathe out. I'm not going to contribute a thing to the plants.' What would happen? Both the cow and the plants would die. The cow has to breathe out, or it'll suffocate. The plant, which can't live without the cow's creating the carbon dioxide it needs, will die as well. Life depends on the recycling of this element through the various stages — plant to animal and back again."

"The same is true of *tzedakah*," Rabbi Hodakov said about giving charity. "It's the same coin that circulates. You use it, give it to someone else, they use it, and it comes back around. That same coin moves around the world — that's the transfer that makes life possible.

"What would you say to the person who says, 'No, that coin is mine! I'm keeping it. I'm not passing it on'?"

JEWISH RECEPTORS

When you study chemistry, you learn that molecules interact with each other because they have the same chemicals on their surface that are compatible with chemicals on another surface. For example, when a sperm cell approaches an ovum, it's not because the sperm falls in love with the ovum, it's all chemical. There's something on the sperm that's looking for a certain receptor.

Sometimes I visualize the undercurrents or subtleties. Sometimes even a certain sound, a certain groan, or a certain word elicits from the other person a flood of memories or emotion.

I think there are Irish receptors. I know there are Jewish receptors — historical, maybe sociological or psychological. It's sometimes the glue that holds people together, holds the community together. Well, you can poison those receptors. Maybe one of the reasons for the disintegration and dissolution of the Jewish community is because these receptors have been replaced or poisoned by other factors. The very concept in Judaism, *Ahavat Yisroel*, according to *Chasidut*, is that a Jewish soul must love another Jew, because both of them share this little bit of Godliness, the Jewish soul. Maybe the stripping away of God from the Jewish community — the so-called enlightenment, which replaced the Jewish love affair with God with a passion for humanity, humanism — has replaced some of these receptors, poisoned the receptors.

FLESH OF OUR FLESH

The Rebbe was discussing cancer.

"Why is there this absolute antipathy to cancer," he asked, "to the extent that we don't even pronounce the name?"

When Jews talk about cancer, most of us call it something else, *that disease*. Of course, it hasn't always been cancer that's been *that disease*. In generations past, it was tuberculosis that was so terrifying no one spoke its name.

But today, it's cancer. Even my son, who works at the Mayo Clinic, says that when he has to tell a patient that cancer is present, he finds himself hedging over either *cancer* or *malignancy*.

Why is that? It's not just the danger, the Rebbe said. Other things are of greater danger to human life. Is it the pain? But other things are equally painful.

No, he said. The antipathy arises because cancer occurs when your own flesh begins to destroy you. With cancer, it's not a foreign body that's invading. It's not a knife cutting. It's not a microbe from outside that's causing your distress. It's that a part of your body has turned destructive. Some of your own cells have gone off, under their own power, and are out of control. Ultimately, your own cells will kill you, if you don't do something.

The hatred for cancer, the incredible fear of the disease, comes about because it's your own body that's attacking itself. You are your own problem. It's not some invading force from outside.

VOLUNTARY VICTIMS

*N*ext to the actual saving of life, compassion for unfortunate victims predominates the hierarchy of Jewish values. Our halachic or legal responsibilities toward widows and orphans, our duties to care for the sick, the poor, and the handicapped, are based directly on biblical commandments. Indeed, the fulfillment of the duties beyond the obligatory halachic standards has become synonymous with Jewish *community* all over the world for thousands of years.

In recent years, however, it is becoming ever more evident that many victims of disease and illness are not really "innocent" victims in the classic sense of being blameless. There is no doubt that they are ill and suffer from their afflictions. They certainly did not harm themselves deliberately, and their condition still elicits our concern and our sympathy.

But there is similarly no doubt that most of the leading causes of illness and death today — including heart disease, certain types of cancer, stroke, highway and home accidents, AIDS, and chronic obstructive pulmonary diseases such as emphysema — result from or are seriously aggravated by preventable behavior patterns and lifestyles.

Moreover, in most of these cases, the "victim" knew about the possible consequences of his or her behavior early enough to modify the risks.

There are many halachic questions associated with the concept of a "voluntary victim." Can the doctor refuse treatment or relegate the voluntary victim to the end of the line? What rights does the person with self-inflicted injury have when medical resources and medicines must be rationed? Is the community or mutual insurance plan obligated to pay for such treatment, particularly if the patient has private resources? Can the community coerce its citizens to modify risk-taking behavior?

Public Health and Divine Punishment

R eally, there are only two kinds of science: good science and poor science. I've always tried to do good science, before, during, and after my stages of indoctrination into Torah and the *mitzvot*, the commandments. Sometimes I succeeded, sometimes not. But my honest belief in the literal truth of every word in the Torah hasn't significantly affected the success / failure ratio of getting funded or getting published. If there is a science–religion conflict, I missed it in both my scientific career and my Torah career.

As I search my memory, I do recall an incident where the science–religion controversy had more than a passing impact on my work. In a class of 120 nursing students, one young woman insisted that the proper "community health" approach to infectious disease should be prayer. On her examination paper she explained clearly that epidemics were divine punishment visited on communities because of their sins.

It is a testable hypothesis and should be studied by epidemiologists. Indeed, it might be the proper answer in a theology course. But it was the wrong answer in my course in public health. The student failed the examination. She appealed on the grounds of my anti-religious bias. She lost the appeal.

HINDSIGHT

I n the 1950s there was an outbreak of penicillin-resistant staphy-
lococci that has continued in the world. One of the real problems
in medicine is that we're running out of antibiotics to control
bacteria because bacteria are changing their resistance.

So while I was giving a talk for Chabad in London, I met with
some epidemiologists and they invited me to take a leave of absence
from the University of Minnesota and spend three or four months
with them learning how the disease is spread in a hospital.

This was a very insidious thing. People go to a hospital to get
cured — that's the whole function of hospitals — and unfortunately,
they become infected in hospitals. Why? Because all the sick people
with disease also come to hospitals.

So these people were doing research on the spread of the infections within the hospital wards, and they invited me to come and
learn their techniques.

Before I left, the Rebbe asked if it would be all right to send him
a protocol of the research that I intended to do, a description of it.
This was cutting edge. I was going to be doing things with people
who were right on the forefront of studying the epidemiology of
antibiotic-resistant bacteria, and I was very proud of the fact that I
was accepted by them. These people are now listed historically as
the great people. One of them was knighted by the queen. Just to be
invited, you become part of history.

So I handed in the protocol to the Rebbe with a certain amount
of pride. I also wanted the Rebbe to be impressed with what I was
able to do. And the Rebbe looked over this thing and he said, "Very,
very good, and though I don't understand most of it — you're an

expert in the field, and I wish you great success" — just as the Rebbe would say — "but if you ask me, I think it might be a little more fruitful to investigate a different field."

I said, "You know, c'mon, you know, Rebbe ..."

"Why don't you try and study why these bacteria become resistant in the first place? If a microbe is susceptible to penicillin and then becomes resistant, how did it become resistant?"

And I thought to myself, "*Oy vey iz mir.*"

First of all, I was so proud of what I was going to do. And I knew what the Rebbe was suggesting would completely change my path in life. I would have to go back and learn a lot of molecular biology and genetics, which didn't really interest me. I was interested in the drama of epidemiology and studying disease transmission to all bacteria. All epidemiologists love the idea. It's like cutting a chain of transmission and solving it. At the end of the day, it's drama. It's what movies are made of. Movies aren't made of the day-by-day drudgery of molecular biology and genetics.

But now, take a look at the Nobel Prizes that were awarded in medicine and physiology in the years that followed. It's all about the molecular biology of disease, of antibiotic resistance. In other words, the Rebbe, in 1969, in 1970, said to me, "Velvl Greene, if you ask me, it would be more fruitful to go into this field because that's the way ..."

I'm no longer just amazed about the Rebbe. Let's just say the Rebbe is greater than life in this respect. And he said it so modestly, "I don't understand the field, I'm probably wrong, you are the expert, *but* if you ask me, I would think ..."

This is a little frightening. It makes shivers go up my back. Maybe I should have done it — maybe. I'm happy with what I did because the Rebbe always said, "I'll give you my *brachah* that you should be successful in this work." And of course, everything is fine, we're happy, I did a good job in England, I learned a lot, we solved some of the epidemics. We didn't solve the basic question, which was what the Rebbe was getting at.

Now, you might not have to be the Rebbe to do it, but it was the Rebbe who said this. It was the old man sitting in Brooklyn who has no qualification in bacteriology at all, who had never taken a course in molecular biology. So you have to stop and think and you have to feel, my God, I'm an idiot, I'm an idiot.

One of the lessons of the Jewish leap year, which makes up the

deficiency between the Lunar Year and the Solar Year ... is to

remind us about the need to make up any possible deficiency in

the past. Clearly if today is as good as yesterday, but no more,

it does not make up any deficiency, nor is it in keeping with

the principle of all things of holiness having to be on the

ascendancy, which for a Jew means steady advancement

in the ascendancy of form over matter, and the spiritual

over the physical.

— *Rabbi Menachem Mendel Schneerson, 1976*

THE REAL PARADOX

It may be significant that the Torah–science controversy is ignored not only in the lab where I work, but also in the *minyan* where I pray. This may be the real paradox. One should expect the issue to explode here, or at least generate acrimony. Consider the scenario: 20 or 30 veteran Israelis — most of them academics, some even world-class scientists, some with rabbinic ordination from rigorous *yeshivot*, and a few who came along later in life, as I did — all praying together or learning at various *shiurim*, talmudic study sessions, that coalesce during the week, or singing *zemirot*, hymns, on Shabbat.

Most come across as pretty sincere in their belief, their observance, their professions. But the classical conflicts don't seem to be very important. The professor of statistics is not visibly disturbed by the probability of miracles. The researcher of anatomy uses the *Shulchan Aruch*, the *Code of Jewish Law*, rather than his textbooks to determine the kosher status of a fowl. The chemist is more concerned with the proper pronunciation of the Torah reading than with the ratio of carbon 14 to carbon 12 in ancient ax handles.

FACE VALUE

How much acrimony would be spared, how much wasted debate about big bangs would be avoided if Rashi's explanation — that the Torah starts with the story of Creation not to provide a cosmological explanation of mechanisms, but rather just to establish the proprietorship of the world and the right of the Proprietor to allocate portions according to His will — were taken at face value!

I once asked a professor of science why he did not tell his

students that from the viewpoint of the relativity theory the

Ptolemaic system could claim just as much validity as the

Copernican. He answered candidly that if he did that, he

would lose his standing in the academic world, since he would

be at variance with the prevalent legacy from the 19th century.

I countered, "What about the moral issue?"

The answer was silence.

— *Rabbi Menachem Mendel Schneerson, 1964*

BEATING A DEAD HORSE

I n every country, in every city — from Australia to Israel to the United Kingdom — the most urgent questions, the most critical challenges, even the most serious disputes, deal with some aspect of the science–religion controversy.

Mostly I lecture about my major interest — public health and infection control — and these topics are accepted with mild interest and without contradiction, even when I challenge traditional and universal attitudes.

What bothers my audience most is that I wear a yarmulke and *arba kanfos*, the traditional four-cornered garment with fringes, and an unrazored beard. My Jewish audience considers that a paradox. Someone who looks and dresses as I do really has no business being a professor of microbiology with a background in exobiology and spacecraft sterilization. I bother them, and they react with questions about science–religion conflicts.

Now, I personally feel that classical science–religion conflicts have as much viability and pertinence as dead horses. I think the issues have been thoroughly debated, analyzed, rationalized, and compromised and that I can contribute very little that is new to the debates.

But I must be wrong. Much of my experience on the Jewish lecture circuit suggests that the dead horse is being resurrected, or that it never really died.

SCIENCE IN SERVICE
OF THE APPETITES

O ne of the more serious impediments to productive debate about science and religion has very little to do with either science or religion. It is, rather, the attempt to use scientific discoveries to justify giving in. Most Jewish non-observant and under-educated Jews consider Torah and *mitzvot* to be inconvenient and burdensome. Still, they are too proud or sensitive to disavow their historical heritage. It just doesn't look right. How can you exhort your children to go to Sunday school or "stay Jewish" if they see that the literal biblical commandments about eating shrimp and turning on the TV during Shabbat are violated? Science to the rescue! Not only can you use science to prove that the kosher dietary laws are old-fashioned health laws no longer relevant, you can also indulge your appetite to be modern simultaneously.

That's a powerful combination. It takes more than logical debate to overcome appetite *and* science *and* one's modern self-image.

It is common knowledge that most Western Jews identify either with no Jewish religious institution or else with those that make minimal personal observance demands (other than a financial commitment and several sessions per year of passive attendance). Perhaps Darwin and Pasteur and Mendel really induced my grandparents to renounce the *mitzvot* of Torah and to seek a religious environment less demanding than the "four *amos*" (cubits) of *Halachah*. It's hard to tell if this is really true.

Our grandparents, parents, and we, ourselves, have used many excuses to liberate ourselves from the yoke of Torah. It if wasn't Darwin, it could have been the Holocaust, or it could have been atomic

energy or heart transplants or the brave new world of Socialism or
Zionism or Ethical Culture. We could always find good, socially ac-
ceptable reasons to surrender to our natural appetites. Freud helped
a lot, too.

But it really demeans science to use it for this purpose. If you
want to eat shrimp, by all means — good appetite. But don't justify
the demands of your gut or your glands by invoking science or the
Holocaust. That's vulgar.

At the risk of not sounding very "scientific," I nevertheless

wish to express my hope that you will also apply your research

work to good advantage in the service of G-d, in accord with

the principle, "Know Him in all thy ways."

— Rabbi Menachem Mendel Schneerson, 1965

CHAPTER 5

OFF THE PATH

When God Became a Concept

A WEAK FOUNDATION

O n Friday, May 26, 2001, the Versailles Event Hall in Jerusalem collapsed during a wedding celebration. It was Israel's worst civil disaster — 23 people were killed and over 400 were injured.

The Versailles Hall was just one of thousands of buildings in Israel constructed by what's known as the Pal-Kal method, an innovative engineering technique in which thin sheets of metal are covered with thin layers of concrete.

Pal-Kal isn't new. It was in use even when I came to Israel in the 1980s. It became enormously popular because it's cheap, lightweight, simple to construct, and easy to modify when you want to add on additional space.

The dangers were known early on. In 1986, the Israel Standards Institute actually banned it from use in Israel. They banned it, yes. But still, thousands of buildings were constructed with it afterward.

Then in 1998, two years before Versailles, the Interior Ministry issued a clear directive to all local authorities, all those who had jurisdiction over approving or licensing buildings. They warned again of the dangers of Pal-Kal and urged remediation.

What happened? Nothing.

So what does all this Pal-Kal discussion have to do with being Jewish in the world today? There's a direct parallel.

In the last 200 years of Jewish life, we've seen some remarkable innovations in what once was a relatively stable structure, built to last the 2,000 years of the diaspora. We Jews also had standards and regulations. We had engineers and supervisors. And up until 200 years ago, it all functioned quite well. Sure, it creaked a little, and from time to time the system was torn down by our enemies. They burned it, tried to destroy it, but it never collapsed of its own weight.

But in the last 200 years we adopted a Pal-Kal construction problem of our own. We switched to some pretty shoddy construction techniques. We became reckless innovators. We were negligent. We weren't paying attention.

Thanks to our intemperate tinkering, we began redefining our terms in a way that was basically unstable and certainly not reliable.

Our renovations had a number of names — secular humanism, Reform, even Reconstructionist. In our attempt to find cheap solutions to modern life, what we did in terms of "reconstruction" amounted to criminal negligence. Whole communities in America were rebuilt in highly dangerous form, by people who weren't qualified to make engineering decisions. Why did we do it? Because the new methods were said to be more modern, cheaper, easier to use. The problem was, they weakened the system at the same time. When additional changes were then desired, it became much easier to do.

So the established building codes of Judaism were violated, over and over again.

What did the regulators do? Not much. Which is the reason I don't put the blame on the Reform and Conservative people at all, but almost entirely on our own Orthodox keepers of the keys. While we sat back and watched it happen, our floors were designed to collapse right under us.

It's not as though we didn't know. For the last hundred years, every good sociologist who's studied the American Jewish community, every group who's commissioned a survey, has found exactly the same thing: There are specific, observable, identifiable factors in modern life that contribute to intermarriage, assimilation, and the abandonment of the Jewish life. Just like building a floor with no supporting pillars, they are just as evident and observable. And what are we doing? Just about the same thing everyone did, once the dangers of Pal-Kal were identified and the method banned. Nothing.

Today, the motivation is to get by with the minimum you have to do to meet the government regulatory standards. That's not too different from the guy who's comfortable in his form of Judaism — have a Christmas tree and celebrate some form of Chanukah. Who do I blame? Him? Or the people who make it seem right, because that's what they do, too?

Of course it's not just in Judaism that shoddy reconstruction has taken place, where support pillars have been removed. It happened in the Catholic church, too, as it has in other religious and social structures. The problem is, when God became a concept, when the Torah became a multiple-choice question, a buffet from which you can pick and choose, disaster was unavoidable. A good place to start is by making sure that when necessary patches and repairs are required, they're made by people qualified to make them.

TORAH SCHOLAR

ecause of the discovery of oil in the Gulf of Mexico, Lafayette, LA, was growing. It had a very decent Jewish community, a couple of hundred families, who all belonged to a Reform temple called Rodef Shalom. They didn't have a rabbi. They had a temple building and a cemetery, and a guy from the Reform seminary came out once a year on Rosh Hashanah or Yom Kippur to give sermons. You can imagine, in a small town we got the worst ones, the ones who stuttered, the ones who were practically illiterate.

In that town, I was the only one who could read and write the Hebrew alphabet because I had studied in the Peretz School, I read Shalom Aleichem, I speak Yiddish. Ah, they thought, we got a *talmid chacham*, a Torah scholar — and believe it or not, they actually hired me as a rabbi. I was making $3,000 a year as a professor, so they offered me another $1,000 to be the rabbi. I put on the robe and I gave sermons and I attended brotherhood week.

Well, I'll tell you, being a rabbi had a lot of privileges, like what *parshah* to read, what *sedrah*, what part of the Torah to read. I went through the Bible once and a lot of it was pretty dull, so I eliminated this, and we never read that. There is some pretty good stuff that comes around after Tisha B'Av — a lot of morality, a lot of human rights, a lot of good things for someone in Louisiana at that time — so we read that part over and over and over. I'd get a hundred people over to a sermon and they all enjoyed that. But then I realized, my little girl, at the age of four, after a year in the Jewish day school, she knew more than I did — and I was the rabbi!

NEW DOESN'T ALWAYS TRANSLATE TO GOOD

D id you know there is a federal Office of Planetary Quarantine? There's even an International Agreement on Planetary Protection. What do all the nations agree to?

Two things, basically:

1. Any country that sends things into space needs to make sure that none of the bad stuff we have here on earth — like diseases — contaminates or infects whatever is up there; and

2. Make sure we don't bring anything back into the common sphere until it's been demonstrated to be safe.

Of course, every country that sends up astronauts violates that agreement. When we sent men to the moon, we were taking a tremendous risk — not only that they'd get blown up or disappear, but no one had any idea what they'd bring back that could be harmful to the rest of us.

There's no two ways about it: Exploring new territory can be hazardous. You have to be very careful not to bring disaster into the new territory, and equally careful you don't bring new calamities back home.

Although it sounds like a truism, it's worth saying that *new* doesn't always translate to *good*, especially when vulnerable young people are involved. When you're raising children, you have to be very careful that your own bad material doesn't destroy the new territory of their minds and bodies. Children are more vulnerable to all sorts of damage — their systems aren't strong enough to resist disease, and in terms of ideas, they haven't developed sufficient wisdom and life experience to assess the potential of the new, good or bad.

The Rebbe used to discuss this concept in the context of an oak tree. Carve something into an old oak tree, he'd say, and the tree will survive. Even if you cut very deeply, the tree is old, hard wood. It has enough substance to go on living, in spite of the wound. But take a young sapling, and put a slight nick in it. For the rest of its existence, there's a flaw in that area. It will never completely disappear.

If I sound like a real stickler, I'm not. I'm not at all against new ideas. I do believe they should be dealt with by people who are well grounded and sufficiently educated and experienced that they won't be overawed. Sometimes a new idea is just that: new. It isn't necessarily good, nor will it stand the test of time.

Similarly, some of us old war horses have developed an immunity to new ideas — we've been there, done that. Even harmful ideas don't hurt us anymore. But that isn't true for someone who hasn't been exposed — a newcomer of any sort.

PILOT CHECK LIST

S ometimes Judaism can be boring.

There's no doubt about it — when you're in a hurry, when you have other things to do, you come to services and just want to get done, so you can go on to other pressing matters.

Even on Yom Kippur, as you go through the service, you see there's a lot of repetition. You're constantly going over things you've gone over before. And let's be honest: There are parts that aren't as exciting as others. We get bored.

Sometimes, to avoid boredom, our rabbis — who don't want us to get bored, who want us to come to services — will cut out parts that were added in later years, in the Middle Ages, during the Crusades. But even at that, we're still going through it all, one by one, and lots of times it seems like we're using the same words: "Blessed are Thou our God …" "It is written …" And we don't know where it was written. We have other things to do. All kinds of things on our minds.

I thought about this one time when I was on a flight, and inadvertently the door to the flight deck was left open. I was flying business class, and I could look in to see what the pilot was doing.

What was the pilot doing? Going through a checklist — doing exactly the same thing he did yesterday, no doubt, checking each thing, one by one, with great diligence.

Why doesn't the pilot get bored? Why doesn't he shorten his checklists? Thin it out a little? "We don't need to worry about this, no one would ever do that, this is a given, this is too old-fashioned, that belongs to a different time …" They could save a lot of time that way. Presumably, pilots have other things to do, too.

But they don't. They go through every item, one by one. So as I sat and watched that pilot, I was praying, "Stay with that checklist. *All* of it."

The pilot was on the same flight I was — flying that same plane. For his own sake as well as mine, that pilot was going over the whole checklist, carefully and thoughtfully.

No matter how boring, how repetitious, how useless it seemed. Every item, every time. Our lives depended on it.

Our Sages declare that "a nice dwelling broadens a person's

mind" and is conducive to greater achievements both

in personal and communal affairs.

— *Rabbi Menachem Mendel Schneerson, 1978*

Dilution to Extinction

When people warn about the loss of Jewish identity — the diminution of numbers of Jews in Western countries like the U.S., Canada, Australia, and England — they run into an old counter-argument.

The loss is not so bad, others say, because, after all, we are increasing the Jewish population in other ways. The Reform movement, for example, has adopted patrilineal descent. So overall, the number of Jews is remaining solid.

But there might still be a problem with that. In chemistry and biology, we learn that one can dilute to extinction.

When you take a sample of microbial suspension that contains a million bacteria and you add one cc, one cubic centimeter, of pure saline, you've reduced the concentration of microbes from a billion to 100,000. If you do another dilution, same process, you dilute from 100,000 to 10,000.

Another, from 10,000 to 1,000, and so forth until you get to one.

When you've diluted to one, you might think that the next dilution would get you to zero, but of course that can't be. Mathematically, you can never dilute to zero. It becomes 1/10th of one microbe. But wait, is that possible? How could you have a tenth of a microbe? You can't, of course.

In 10 cc's, you can have one microbe; if you dilute that tenfold, it becomes a hundredth of a microbe, which can't be. Instead, it's one microbe in a 100 cc's. If you look at that flask, it's not sterile, it has one microbe. But 99 of the cc's have no microbes in them. It's a phenomenon when you're using particulates in a continuous flow — you can never get to zero.

But you can dilute it to extinction.

Sooner or later, you can make it so that in Minneapolis, there will be no Jews. Or in Minnesota. Or it could be that in the United States, there would be no Jews.

You can never get to zero, because Jews will always survive. But I have no problem explaining to the board of directors of a synagogue that the Jewish content of their community can be diluted to the extent that it is essentially not significant.

THE SIGNAL

J ews are accused of having a deep sense of guilt. We certainly support a large number of social workers, sociologists, and psychologists to relieve us of our guilt. So here's my analogy: I once had an attack on the trigeminal nerve — one of the most painful things a human can experience. Trigeminal neuralgia is so painful that the patients often commit suicide. The ultimate end to preventing suicide is that some doctors do a neurotomy, they cut the nerve. It interferes with chewing, seeing, and smelling, but you're not constantly in pain.

This leads to a question: Why, when a Jewish child is eight days old, do we circumcise him? Instead of circumcision, why don't we go ahead and cut various nerves that might cause pain for him in the future? We could give a person a life free of pain!

The answer is, yes, we could give him a life free of pain, but much of the pain that we suffer from is a warning signal that something is happening. You put your hand on a hot stove, and immediately your nerves say take it away. It hurts! But it's not the pain that's the most important thing here. If you don't take it away, your hand will be destroyed. The pain is a signal to take your hand away.

So is it possible that guilt is a signal that you're doing something you shouldn't be doing?

WHISTLING IN THE SYNAGOGUE

There's an old, old story about a kid raised in a very non-Jewish environment in a small town in Russia. He had absolutely no learning, no background in Judaism, and had never even been in a *shul*, a synagogue, before. When he was maybe nine or ten years old, he was discovered by a visiting Jewish merchant, who saw the kid's potential and took him along to a Jewish community.

The day they arrived was Rosh Hashanah. The kid sat in *shul*, he heard the *chazan*, the cantor, heard the bleat of the *shofar*, heard the congregation *davening*, pouring out their hearts to God. His soul was touched to its very core, and he longed to do something to express himself.

What could he do? He didn't know the language, the ritual, or even how to read. But as a Russian peasant, he knew very well how to whistle. So he put his fingers to his mouth and cut forth with a crashing noise the best whistle he'd ever made.

The congregation was horrified — "*Sha!*" — trying to shut him up. The decorum for this holiest of days was being ripped apart.

But then the rebbe saw what was happening. This pure soul was crying out to God in the finest way it possibly could. The boy's whistle, he said, was equal to whatever everyone else had accomplished that day. The boy's whistle had come straight from his soul.

That's a very nice story, isn't it? But what happens after that?

I have some thoughts — my own rest of the story.

Let's suppose the little Russian boy is now 11 years old, and he's been in the heart of that fervent Jewish community for two years. He's gone to *cheder*, to religious school, he's learned Torah, he's been to *shul* every day for all the prayers. He's been present for all the holidays, in the heart of that beautiful community.

Rosh Hashanah arrives again, and once more, he puts his fingers to his mouth and cuts loose with an ear-splitting whistle.

In fact, for the rest of his life, that's all he does.

Sooner or later, isn't it time for someone to tell him there's a better way?

Try to live up to the principle of the Mishna: "Saying little,

but doing much." The intent of it is surely not "little" per se,

but by comparison to the doing; and that the doing itself

should become "little" by comparison with the next

accomplishment, and so on.

— *Rabbi Menachem Mendel Schneerson, 1976*

SEWAGE IS 99.8 PERCENT PURE WATER

The word *sewage* has a very bad connotation. Who likes sewage?

But still, sewage happens. It's a part of reality that's impossible to escape. If there's a person, family, or community, there will be sewage.

The thing about sewage is that it's defined as liquid waste, the stuff that runs in drains. So of course someone analyzed it — engineers have to figure out how to get rid of it, so they need to know what it is.

What they found is that sewage is 99.8 percent pure water. Only .2 percent is actually the objectionable, putrid, infectious, disgusting material we all despise.

So 99.8 percent is pretty pure — even better than Ivory Soap, which is 99.44 percent.

So if it's purer than Ivory Soap, why don't we wash with sewage? Why don't we drink sewage? Why not? It's 99.8 percent pure!

Why not? Because it's .2 percent sewage, that's why. And the .2 percent is seriously foul.

It's just the same as when people tinker with Jewish traditions.

Even though they might be 99.8 percent based on fundamental Jewish tradition, they're 99.8 percent Torah centered, God centered, 99.8 percent in compliance with *Halachah*, the problem is that .2 percent.

That .2 percent is still foreign. That means it's still sewage.

THE STANDARD METHOD

During research into the microbiology of the stratosphere, we employed large helium-filled balloons that carried our samples to altitudes of 20,000 feet. During the occasional successful flight, we were able to recover from the stratosphere a few milligrams of dust, which we transported with great care to the laboratory for bacteriological analyses. Here we had a lot of advice. Everyone had his opinion about the procedure for the analyses — but I only had these few milligrams of dust. I only had these few precious samples.

Behind my desk is a series of manuals titled *Standard Methods*. There are *Standard Methods for Dairy Products Analysis* and *Standard Methods for Water Analysis* and even *Standard Methods for Micro-Biological Analysis of Spacecraft Hardware*. The methods are basically undramatic. There is very little flamboyance about them. They have only one major attribute: They have a high probability of working. The standard methods are reviewed every so often and new methods are incorporated. But before acceptance, each method must be tested and tested and retested against the previous methods and must be shown to work at least as well.

If I had a lot of samples, and a lot of time, and a lot of money, I would certainly have taken all of the advice — advice given with the best of intentions. But I had only these precious samples, and any mistake was irrevocable. I analyzed my samples by the standard methods.

My wife and I think of our children as precious samples. We want to educate them according to Torah guidelines, the standard method for our people. The Torah might not be flamboyant or dramatic, but it has withstood the test of time and experience. Our precious samples are too few for experimentation. There is no absolute guarantee that the standard methods will work. But the accumulated experience of several thousand years suggests that there is no other way.

When it comes to the theory of evolution, dealing with an effort to reconstruct the distant past, science lacks even that degree of probability which it has in regard to future predictions ... here science can only speculate. If such speculations are represented in text-books as "facts," then it is a gross and unscientific misrepresentation.

— Rabbi Menachem Mendel Schneerson, 1964

THE DIFFERENCE BETWEEN SIGNAL AND NOISE

$\mathcal{N}$ot too many people have heard about Project Ozma. This was an attempt by the National Aeronautics and Space Administration to detect the presence of intelligent life on other planets by cosmic communication. A massive radio-telescope, located in West Virginia, was focused toward some predetermined stars, and the operators listened.

No one outside the field of cosmic communication is quite sure about what they expected to hear. But we are told that the rationale behind the program was not as fantastic as it appeared to the layman. If there was intelligent life out there, the argument went, and if their electronic communication apparatus was equal to or better than ours, and if they were as curious about life on earth as we were about life on their planet, they would try to signal us.

And it appears that sophisticated electronics people are not inhibited by any language barrier — they communicate by means of numbers. After all, anyone who can build a transmitter would have the same kind of mathematical tools as anyone who could build a receiver. Thus our people listened. They were listening for a signal that was non-random, that was repeated, that had a consistent rhythm or numerical code, and that occurred at specific time periods.

This much is true. The remainder is probably apocryphal, but the story persists. It has been told that only a few months after Project Ozma was initiated, the operators became very excited. Everything they were listening for was present. At very specific times of the day a faint signal was heard. The signal was quite unintelligible

— at least it bore no resemblance to any language or code in the lexicon of the listeners — but it was there. It wasn't ordinary random static or noise, it was repeated with some minor variation at different periods, and it had a definite but somewhat unearthly beat.

Fortunately, before announcing this great discovery to the world, the scientists checked and rechecked their data. They then found that because of a slight aberration in the radio-telescope's focus, they were not communicating with outer space at all, but were picking up a strong signal from a rock-and-roll radio station in Kentucky.

The story has a meaning to those in the Jewish community who are also concerned with a type of cosmic communication. We are also listening intently for some type of signal, and we experience all kinds of frustration and difficulty with our electronics:

• There are those who have the wireless turned off completely and deny that there is any sound at all.

• There are those who are sincerely turned on, but will listen only to what they want to hear and refuse to switch channels.

• There are those whose signal is confused by static or electronic noise, and thus can never gain the full appreciation of the signal itself.

• There are those whose signal is completely drowned out by noise, and they are frustrated because their ears tell them that they are not listening to anything meaningful.

• There are those who have heard only static all their lives and assume that what they hear is a signal. They are quite adamant in refusing when someone wants to help them re-adjust the set, since they are quite happy with the noise.

• And fortunately, there are those who by tradition know what to listen for, and by training know how to adjust the set. They can filter out the noise and receive pure signals.

Some people fall into the latter fortunate category by nature. Most of the rest of us have to learn — to learn the difference between signal and noise, and to learn how to tune in properly.

SPECTATOR OR PARTICIPANT?

In Lafayette, LA, the university invited one of the Nobel Prize winners to speak. To summarize, he spoke about glycolysis, the process of breaking down carbohydrates. He gave a public lecture to the faculty, and because Nobel laureates were very, very rare in Lafayette, LA, everyone was invited. Even the spouses of the scientists came.

To those of us who knew something about the subject, it was very interesting. But Gail was there, God bless her. I don't know why she came — there wasn't much of a social life around there. After it was finished, I felt sorry that she had come, because I'm sure she had become unalterably bored.

So I asked her, "Did you understand anything that he said?"

And she said, "Of course. Glucose. Is that sugar?"

I said yes. And I felt sorry. She understood one word.

And then I thought to myself, so who enjoyed that lecture? The faculty who knew some chemistry. Who enjoyed it even more? The faculty who knew he won the Nobel Prize. And who really enjoyed the lecture? The people who read some seminal papers the week before he came. Those people were glowing. And some who came knew only that glucose was sugar.

It's the same at any synagogue on a Shabbos morning, or on Yom Kippur or Rosh Hashanah. A lot of people come, and all they get out of it is that glucose is sugar.

But then there's the guy who knows something about the reading of the Torah itself. And another who knows more. And the ones who went over it three times — that's what the Torah says, you go over it three times with Rashi. Watch that on Shabbos. They not only aren't bored — they are correcting the person reading it. They're leading.

I once asked Gail if she gets bored during her rehearsals. She did a lot of Mozart. I like Mozart. I like *Don Giovanni*, but quite honestly, I don't think I can watch *Don Giovanni* more than a few times a year.

So I asked Gail, "OK, so I can watch *Don Giovanni* three or four times a year. You rehearse every day. You practice, and you never seem to be bored. What is it about you that's different from me?"

"Oh, that's easy," she says. "You're a spectator, and I'm a participant. Every time I sing it, I try to put myself into it. I am part of it. You — you are sitting on a hard bench trying to be entertained."

COMING DOWN FROM SINAI

The narrative in the Torah about the Shavuot story, the giving of the Torah to the Jews on Mount Sinai, is absolutely amazing, if you read it carefully. This was a moment that had never occurred before in the history of creation, and will never occur again. You can look at it in a simple way, just the story itself: Here's God communicating directly with man, His creation.

Here is the Ultimate in Spirituality in actual contact with the ultimate in materialism — and they're communicating. Even the environment was completely unique: It was entirely quiet, no sound at all other than the words of God. Maybe that's a miracle in itself. All 600,000 Jews together, and they were quiet?

So the smoke was billowing, and the mountain rumbling, and all the Jews sat there quietly, listening. What a fantastic experience. It has to be one of the greatest events in the history of the world. We heard God talking.

And then it's over. The mountain stops rumbling, the smoke disappears, Moshe Rebbenu, Moses, ascends to the mountain to get the written copy, the verification of what he heard. And slowly, the people start coming down from this ultimate in spiritual highs. They wander off.

At some point, they must have started talking to each other. What do you think the first words said were? I don't know for sure, but I suspect that some guy is going to turn to his wife and say, "What's for supper?" That's what guys do — they're hungry, and they want to know what's for supper.

But this time, the question was monumental. Indeed, what was for supper?

His wife couldn't give her family leftovers — the world had changed. She couldn't even use the pots and pans she'd used before. The question, "What's for supper?" was simple, but the answer is, "You can't do what you did before. You can't eat what you did before. You can't live like you did before."

I have friends who are of the Reform/Conservative persuasion, who sometimes accuse the Orthodox of what they call *pots and pans Judaism*. "You've taken a beautiful, spiritual religion," they say, "and all you can focus on is pots and pans. There's all this gorgeous spiritual material there — be kind to your neighbor, be good to animals — revolutionary stuff! And what have you done with it? You've turned it into this much milk and that much meat. Into kosher and not kosher. This pot and not that one. How silly is that?"

But you see, that's what Mount Sinai was all about. There was this momentous spirituality, this incomparable meeting between man and God, but at the end of the day the question is, "What's for supper?"

We never discard the spiritual moments, but ultimately that's how it plays out in our daily lives, "What's for supper?"

RAIN IN THE DESERT

Life was harried when we first moved to Israel. I was stressed out, feeling hassled and distracted over a lot of things — our absorption process, my new job, how the family was adjusting. I had so many things to do, and not enough time. Among other things, we were preparing our son for his *bar mitzvah*, so things were hectic.

I didn't always have time to go to *shul* in the mornings, so I'd *daven* by myself at home. I remember this one morning — it was a Friday, in the winter, so it was a short day — and I had so many things to do, a whole list. I really didn't have time to pray, so I was rushing through it as fast as I could.

On top of everything else, it was raining, which would do nothing more than make all my errands harder yet. We didn't have a car, so rain was a big issue.

I came to the *Kriat Shma*, the reading of *Shma*. There, in that second paragraph, are the words, "… and I shall provide rain for your land in its proper time, the early and the late rains, and you shall gather in your grain, and your wine, and your oil."

There I was, praying those words. In Israel. In Beersheva, where it rains very rarely. This was the prayer set forth by God to bring rain to the desert, right here to us, when we needed it. In Israel, rain is the biggest blessing we can find — and there I was, wishing it would stop.

I had a lot of things to do. It was raining. I wanted it to stop.

But at the same time I was praying for rain. That was the paradox.

Fortunately, I caught myself, and decided I'd better get with it.

Which of these prayers was I really making? What was I really asking for? Rain? Or the convenience of staying dry while I ran my errands?

Which one are you asking for?

THE ROAD BACK

The Rebbe calls the youth of today the *lost generation*. They're far from the path of Torah, far from *Halachah*, Jewish law. As far as we can see, they're lost.

Imagine you're walking along a highway and you find yourself in the middle of a forest. Now be honest, he says. Highways don't turn into forests instantly. Somehow, you left that highway, one step at a time.

You walked to the edge of the road. Then you took another step, then another. You didn't suddenly find yourself lost in the forest — you got there gradually. It was a process, a slow process.

Now, you can come back; you can do it slowly and gradually if you want. The Torah spells it all out, that's the Guidelines.

Just remember, when you're lost, you didn't get lost suddenly. You lost yourself, slowly and gradually. But you can come back all at once.

The Basis of Jewish Identity

I n today's common usage, the adjective *Jewish* is not much more than an ethnic or behavioral trait that permits rapid cataloguing of such things as restaurants, TV characters, or voter blocks. Often it is nothing more than an ad hoc judgment or pronouncement by someone who calls himself or herself *rabbi, spokesperson, activist,* or *authority.* It is no surprise. In the context of Jewish history this is a relatively new question and today everyone is an expert on all things Jewish.

Not too long ago, the use of the adjective *Jewish* was more carefully circumscribed. It would imply that it was created by Jews, was of vital concern and interest to Jews, and was recognizable as such by both Jews and non-Jews (like the duck who is recognized to be a duck because it walks like one, quacks like one, and looks like one).

Philosophers and historians may debate *Jewish identity* today, but most Jewish ideas or institutions or moral systems of merit are identifiable as such: vertically, through succeeding Jewish generations in history; and horizontally, as relevant across geographical and cultural lines in the present world. And a major criterion for recognizing these as Jewish is their fundamental origin in Torah and its 613 *mitzvot.*

CHAPTER 6

THE REBBE

There Is an Old Man in Brooklyn Who Thinks About You

THREE REBBES

People quite often ask about the Rebbe and I say, really, there are three Rebbes. There is what we call the *Rebbe*, the world-famous figure, the one on the picture, the one who is so famous.

And then, from a chasidic point of view, there is *our Rebbe*, the Rebbe we go to, to ask for advice and for a *brachah*, for a blessing, and to cry on his shoulder.

And then there is a third Rebbe, there is *my Rebbe*; the relationship between the Rebbe and Gail and myself, a young couple, who were actually living and growing up, getting closer and closer to him, as a person, as a teacher, but above all, as a friend.

NACHAS

I had a very good job offer and I wanted very much to take that job, so I came to ask the Rebbe and he said, "No, I think you should stay where you are."

So I said, "If I take the job, Rebbe, will you give me a *brachah*, a blessing, at the very least?"

He said, "I have already given you a *brachah*. I gave you a *brachah* for *nachas*, joy, from children. What other *brachah* can there be?"

It brings tears to my eyes.

So from then on, when we look at our children — our children and grandchildren and great-grandchildren — I see what a *brachah* is. It's nearly enough to make you religious. It's nearly enough to make you a *Chasid*.

It is … quite natural for a person to gain encouragement in
direct proportion to the success of his efforts, and there is
no end to the good, so that when a person has done his
maximum one day, G-d provides additional capacities for
even greater effort and accomplishment the next day.

— *Rabbi Menachem Mendel Schneerson, 1968*

DIVINE INSIGHT

We developed this remarkable friendship toward this man — not the prophet, not the greatest scholar, not the leader of this worldwide movement, but this friend. On our 10th wedding anniversary — he asked us to come in 1966 — again, he stood up and held the chair, and when we left, he took us to the door.

I asked him, "Would you give us a blessing, would you give us a blessing?"

He said, "I'll give you a blessing: You should have *nachas* from your children, Jewish *nachas* from your children. And you'll do me a favor" — we should do the Rebbe a favor — "you should remember that there is an old man in Brooklyn who thinks about you, and my *brachah* is to come back on your 20th anniversary."

In chasidic terms, this is an invitation. We've got 10 years to do this. This is why I say there's a difference between the various levels of appreciation of the Rebbe. What the Rebbe writes in a letter sometimes is something that is absolutely appropriate to the whole world. Most of the time, on the other hand, it's basically a very nice, gentle criticism of me for not writing letters, not sending reports.

The Rebbe always asked for reports from me. In fact, one day, in a moment of exasperation, I was in the Rebbe's office, and the Rebbe said, "You owe me a report." I was being a little flippant — excuse me for saying so, but you want the truth — so I said to him, "They say that the Rebbe has *ruach hakodesh*, the Rebbe has this divine insight to see things. So if the Rebbe has *ruach hakodesh*, why is he asking me for a report? Doesn't he know what's going on?"

You know, *Chasidim* would slap me. The Rebbe didn't slap me.

The Rebbe smiled and he said in Yiddish, "*Vos men zogt, zol men zuggen*. What they say, let them say. From you, I want a report."

This is the kind of personal thing that I'll never forget. I'll never forget.

CONFIDENCE IN THE CREATOR

The Rebbe wrote Gail two letters after two of the miscarriages. They were marked private for Gail. What the Rebbe said, Gail told me, was not to give up hope; to have faith, but that everything is in the hands of the creator of good and the one who creates good can do nothing but create good, so everything is going to be OK. That's what he said.

He advised her, "Continue what you're doing, but when you *bentch licht,* before you light the candles on Shabbos, have a coin box and put a few coins in it."

This is a normal thing; we'd do it anyway, we give *tzedakah,* charity. And the Rebbe told her, "Just have confidence."

Until the pregnancy has entered into the fifth month, the matter

should be kept confidential except in regard to the closest relatives.

It is also customary to have the Tefillin and Mezuzoth checked,

to make sure they are Kosher, if this has not been done within

the past twelve months. [It is also] the custom of Jewish

women to put aside a small coin for Tzedoko before lighting

the candles Erev Shabbos and Erev Yom Tov.

— *Rabbi Menachem Mendel Schneerson, 1970*

WORDS OF WISDOM

I f you were to ask me now, in my old age, what the Rebbe teaches, it's *Toras Moshe*, it's Torah that you might not agree with it — but you can't ignore it.

The weekly portion of the Torah should be a source of timely inspiration and instruction to every Jew, in all affairs of that week. Mattan Torah (the giving of the Torah) has the further significance in that it has to be regarded and accepted as a new experience every day. This is also evidenced from the Brocho (blessing) over the Torah which we make every morning in our morning prayers — noten hatorah, Giver of the Torah — in the present tense. Our Sages declared that the words of the Torah should be as new every day.

— *Rabbi Menachem Mendel Schneerson, 1964*

SELF-SACRIFICE

The Rebbe was very interested in how Gail saw the young Jewish girls being raised in Russia — whether there was an opportunity to be raised as a Jewish girl or whether the Communists were having too much influence. Gail told him what she saw, that the Chabad families were really struggling.

It made him cry. He cried for the *mesiras nefesh*, for the self-sacrifice of all these people, for everyone who maintained *Yiddishkeit* in Russia at that time.

THE REBBE'S REPRESENTATIVES

O ur greatest influences were from personal contacts with the Rebbe's *shluchim*. The incidents with the Rebbe were several times a year when we got to see him, several times a year we got a letter, but the rest of the time, we were under the influence of a *shaliach*, a person sent out to spread the Rebbe's knowledge.

Imagine — imagine taking young couples, basically a *yeshiva* boy and a girl who went to Bais Rivkah. They get married. They want to be at home, they're more comfortable in Crown Heights or Boro Park, but they're sent to Bratislava, Anchorage, small towns in New Mexico, Hong Kong, Argentina, Africa.

We were very impressed by the *shluchim*. A very special breed of person becomes a *shaliach*. These young men and women will be the story of the 20th century, every bit as much as the old stories of the early Zionist *chalutzim*, the pioneers, or the soldiers who fought in the War of Independence and any part of Jewish history.

CONSIDERATION

The Rebbe's great concern was how our children were — their education, how they were growing. His great concern was Gail — whether she was going along with the fact that this was taking an awful lot of my time. He wanted to know because he understood this was taken from her. She had one husband and her husband was very rarely home, even on a Shabbos.

So the Rebbe always used to ask her, does she mind that Chabad is taking so much of the time that really belongs to her. It was a very, very thoughtful type of thing.

PROPHECY

T here are things that the Rebbe said back in 1963 that are as relevant today as any *nevua*, any prophecy, made by our *neviim*, by our prophets.

The so-called scientific arguments which purport to deny the

possibility of the Torah account of Creation are not *scientific,*

since in truth science does not, and cannot, make such a claim.

Moreover, modern science declares that it can never *offer an*

unequivocal scientific solution to this and similar problems.

The reason for this is not that modern science is still

incomplete, but rather because of the very nature of science

which can never speak in absolute terms; it can only offer

working theories and hypotheses. Science can only examine

and classify phenomena, and make probable *deductions*

and predictions. If these are eventually substantiated by

experiment, the theories are confirmed as approximate verities.

But never can science claim to speak in terms of absolute

truths, for it could be a contradiction in itself.

— *Rabbi Menachem Mendel Schneerson, 1964*

WHICH IS MORE IMPORTANT?

The Rebbe once referred to Jewish college professors as a *black hole*. At one time, they could have been light, they could have been a source of illumination, but they have collapsed on themselves to such an extent that not only do they not give any light, but any light that goes through them is absorbed and it remains a black hole.

There are infinite stories the Rebbe told in this respect. Maybe this is a good time to say it. There were a number of times that I was going to give a talk, either to B'nai B'rith, Jewish scientists, even university people, when the Rebbe said, "I'd like you to give over a certain thought, but please don't mention my name, don't tell them in my name."

According to Torah, when you tell over something, you should tell it over in someone's name. One of the ways of bringing *Moshiach*, the Messiah, is telling it over. But the Rebbe said, "Don't bring it in my name." Why? "Because," he said, "it's much more important that they learn the lesson, that they learn this particular Torah, than that I get credit for it."

A CANNIBAL IN THE OBSERVATION TOWER

Let us imagine, the Rebbe said, that a cannibal from one of the Samoa Islands — Pago Pago, maybe — develops a life-threatening illness. The doctor who attends him says surgery is essential if we're to save his life, so they put the cannibal on an airplane and fly him to a very modern hospital. He has a friend with him — another cannibal — who of course can't go into the operating room, but is shown to an observation room where he can watch the whole thing.

The cannibal watches while his friend is wheeled in, naked, strapped to a narrow board. Four or five completely masked people come in and pick up sharp knives. His sick friend doesn't seem to see any of this; he's strapped down and apparently unconscious, with something over his own mouth. Then the masked men begin cutting on him.

Now this cannibal knows exactly what those masked men are doing to his friend — he has a personal cultural affinity with this process. He knows his friend is being carved up for one purpose only.

Try telling him that those men with knives are helping his friend, not killing him. Try to convince him his friend will be healthier than before, that they're saving his life, not ending it.

He will never believe you. All he knows is cannibalism.

The Rebbe used this as an example of human suffering in our own lives. We suffer, and we ask God, "Why are you doing this? Why are you torturing me? Why are we being cut up?" Because what we understand is torture and cutting up.

Try to convince us that what God is doing is actually for our own benefit. That He's saving us, not killing us.

We have to really struggle if we're going to see that.

Between Purim and Pesach, the role of the Jewish woman is

brought to mind with especial emphasis, as is evidenced by the

fact that the Megillah of Purim is called not after Mordecai,

nor after Mordecai and Esther jointly, but after Esther alone

— Megillas Esther. Similarly, in connection with Pesach, our

Sages declare that it was in the merit of the righteous women

in those days that our ancestors were delivered from Egypt.

Our festivals are not simply reminders of events in the past, but

rather guideposts for the present and future, inasmuch as the

Torah is eternal. Indeed, since the road has been paved, the going

is much easier now for the Jewish women to carry out their im-

portant role in Jewish life. Thus the present time of year is partic-

ularly auspicious and stimulating for Jewish women and

daughters, both in their personal and family life, as well as to

serve as an inspiring example to the environment at large. More-

over, we have the assurance of our Sages that "One who is deter-

mined to purify oneself, and others, received aid from On High."

— Rabbi Menachem Mendel Schneerson, 1971

LOYALTY

I'm very concerned when people talk about the observant Jew who's so involved with minutia and casuistry. Everything is regulated by inches — you don't make a blessing on the bread unless you eat the size of an olive or an egg. Measurements. Shabbat comes at 7:19 and after that you don't light the candles — this can tie us up in knots.

The king of England and the czar of Russia and the kaiser of Germany were having an argument as to whose soldiers were the most loyal.

The king of England, to demonstrate loyalty, called in the captain of the guard, who is the top officer. He said, "Will you obey me if I give you an order?"

The captain said, "Of course, absolutely!"

So the king said, "Jump out the window!"

Third story building! The captain said, "But your majesty! I have a wife, a family! How is this possible?"

Dismissed! The other two were laughing — this is loyalty?

The kaiser said, "I'll show you!" So he called in his captain of the guard, and they went through the same dialogue.

"Who are you?"

"The captain of the guard."

"Who am I?"

"You're the kaiser."

"Will you obey me? Will you do anything I say?"

"Absolutely!"

"Jump out the window!"

"Yes, sir," and he jumped out the window.

They applauded that. It was really good. How could you beat that?

So the czar called in his captain, and again the same dialogue."

"Who are you?"

"The captain of the guard."

"Who am I?"

"The czar."

"Jump out the window!"

"Yes, sir. Which window?"

That's loyalty.

The Rebbe says we think sometimes that *mesiras nefesh*, self-sacrifice, means jumping from the roof, tearing your hair out, screaming wildly. No, no, no. If you're going to sacrifice yourself for something, you need to know exactly how and who and when. This is *miseras nefesh* — to know which window, otherwise you're just jumping out windows.

ARMOR

The Rebbe once described an interesting paradox regarding danger: There was a soldier, he said, who was experienced in battle. On coming home to his own house, his own chair, he'd put on his armor. When he left the house to go out into the world, he'd take the armor off.

Does that make any sense? Hardly. So then how is it that some Jews decide they will only wear a *kippah* and *tzitzit* when they're at home — and take them off when they leave the house?

Where do you need the armor? In your home, or out there in the world?

EPILOGUE

*Is the Torah–Science Debate
Still an Issue?*

Within the last couple of years, someone found a rock in the Antarctica. This rock, they said, came from Mars. They cut it open, and lo! — inside were what they said were microbes, or "microbe-like structures." On this, they have fashioned a whole new science of the microbiology of life on Mars.

This is complete nonsense.

Today's world is filled with imaginary situations — there are books and TV, children's programs, the whole world of show business. The trouble is, some people believe it. I spent a large segment of my life working with the questions of life in outer space, and I can tell you this: We don't have a clue whether there is or was life of any kind on Mars.

So tell me you've found this rock that has microbes from Mars? We don't know. That's the only honest statement we can make.

Why is this relevant? Because it replicates the whole recurring controversy that pits science against religion — or better stated, science against Torah. I'd better stay away from the *religion* word because I'm certainly not an authority on middle 19th-century Anglican theology, which is where all the controversy originated. Science's argument with Darwin — assuming there is one — didn't come from our rabbis. It came from the bishops of the Anglican church. Prior to that, it was the pope and the Catholic church who had a problem with Galileo. Not the rabbis.

Is there still a debate between Torah and science? Does anyone out there still believe the Torah story? Indeed they do. And that's the reason it's become such a hot political issue. I'm always amazed when I give a talk in, say, Anchorage, AK, on a November night, when it's 30 below zero. Why would people leave their warm homes and come out to listen to somebody like me? Hardly any of them were Jews, and yet on that icy night, over 200 people were interested in what I had to say. OK, maybe there's not a lot to do in Anchorage on a November night, but still. You'd think there must have been something on television.

The Torah–science debate still fascinates people — not just Jews or fundamentalist Christians, either. It tugs at some basic element of conscience, pulling one way or the other. It makes you want to know how the problem is resolved.

There are some groups who aren't affected: Most of my very religious friends dismiss the issue easily. For them, the Torah is true. Period. Whatever doesn't agree with the Torah is irrelevant, not worth thinking about. They don't really care about various scientific theories on how old the world is, or about dinosaurs or evolution.

For them, the Torah itself is the bottom line.

A segment of my secular friends are equally untroubled. For them, science is true. Period. The Torah? Well, that's some kind of allegory. It doesn't have anything to do with fact.

Most Jews I know solve this problem handily, in one of two ways. One group finds a compromise. "Science tells us how the heavens move," they say. "Religion tells us how to move the heavens."

Isn't that nice and pat? Science tells us how, Torah tells us why. They live in two worlds at the same time.

Another group manages it by compartmentalization. They would say, "When I'm in the classroom giving a lecture, I teach science, the way it's done at Harvard. When I'm in the *shul* on Yom Kippur, I pay no attention to science. In synagogue, I believe in God. I take the Torah literally. I worry about what Abraham was going to do with his son Ishmael."

But there's a huge gap in congruency. How can they do that, and have inner peace?

Why can't all of us live in a world of compromise and/or compartmentalization? The answer is complex, but starts with the fact that the Torah forbids it. In terms of compartmentalization, the Christian theology is the forerunner: "Render unto Caesar that which is Caesar's," Jesus said, "and unto God that which is God's."

In relation to compromise, the Torah equally forbids that: For Jews, one of our most fundamental dogmas is, "There is nothing other than God." No parallel theories or entities are permitted.

So neither compromise nor compartmentalization is compatible with Torah.

The fact of the controversy causes real problems. Unfortunately, the Torah–science debate is used by Jews — Jews who should know better — as an excuse.

Suppose there's a boy who grew up in the *yeshivah* world. All his life he's kept kosher, he's been chaste, he honored Shabbat. And then he discovers a whole new world in science — and this he gets from the authority of a professor, who takes fees for it! The boy also discovers that he has both hormones and appetites. But everything he's been taught is that it's not nice to satisfy your appetites — you're a glutton! And it's not nice to satisfy your hormones — you're a libertine!

So what he does is allow science to cast the original Torah narrative — based on some distant past somewhere — and reclassify it as legend. Now, satisfying your appetites and your hormones really isn't such a bad thing. The only thing that prohibits it is a dusty old book based on ancient legends. You may as well put away your *tefillin*.

True, that doesn't happen very often. Not many men put away their *tefillin* because they've discovered Darwin. But there are plenty who don't put them on in the first place because even if they felt an urge to do so, they resist. That would be a concession. It would be betraying Darwin and science and the Harvard School of Paleontology. Can't have that!

So let's rephrase the question: Do the scientific discoveries of the last 200 years sufficiently contradict and invalidate the narrative of Torah to authoritatively cast doubt on its authenticity?

That's the crux of the argument: If science contradicts the narrative of Torah, then it also contradicts the moral rulings of Torah.

Does it do that?

In the world of contrast and compare, it's a little dicey. Science doesn't accept concepts like soul or sin, good or evil. Concepts like morality and faith and spirituality cannot be dealt with in science, because they can't be measured or quantified. That being the case, in science, they simply have no validity. But assuming we can come up with some comparable concepts, there are some elemental conclusions we can reach.

After years of suffering through this issue myself, after my own dark nights of the soul, pondering how these concepts interact — or don't — here are four conclusions I've reached:

1. The debate between science and Torah is real — but it's essentially foreign to authentic Judaism. True science and true Torah don't contradict each other most of the time.

2. There may never be an all-fours reconciliation because the debate isn't so much about truth as it is about winning.

It would take an awesome amount of truth for a Harvard professor to back down and acknowledge the truth of Torah. It would take an equal amount of evidence for a number of Torah scholars to admit that we must look at what science has to say and examine the conclusions. It's not enough for one side to just knock the other.

3. Most of the conflicts between science and Torah are more apparent than real. There's any number of religious scientists as well as a sizeable group of avowed secularists who are not bothered by any apparent contractions at all. They don't see any significant problem.

And therefore I come to my ultimate conclusion.

4. The basic issues at stake are not the ones you're reading about in the newspaper, or the arguments alleged on both sides about what kind of education should be provided in schools.

In support of my conclusions, I also assert that there's a tremendous ignorance about both science and Torah among the people who are heavily involved in the debate. And that people with varying private agendas are using the Torah–science debate to advance their own particular positions.

Let's examine the ignorance of science:

It's important to understand that the average layman has no real idea about what science can do and what it can't do. He doesn't understand either science or the scientific method.

Even among scientists, however, there's an acute ignorance about any scientific fields other than their own. The problem is caused by increasing specialization and the profusion of knowledge.

I use myself as an example: In my time, I was a pretty good microbiologist. I hold the certification. I passed all the tests. I was elected to office by my peers. I taught on the post-graduate level for 55 years. But to tell you the truth, I've so concentrated my research, so focused my attention on such a tiny area — hospital infection control, methods of disinfection and sterilization — that when I pick up the *Journal of Bacteriology*, or even the *Journal of Applied Microbiology*, of which I was an editor — I can only understand about half the titles. That's the kind of ignorance we're talking about.

If I'm that limited in my own field, what do you think I know about chemistry? Psychology? Geology? Ecology?

So when I'm on a platform talking about science, that's almost laughable. I can't even talk about my own scientific field and its attitude to Torah because I'm so specialized I don't know even half of my own field.

Back in the days of the Renaissance, men like Leonardo da Vinci and Frances Bacon could actually be "Renaissance men" — they could have a smattering of knowledge about most of science as it existed at their time. But today, there is no such thing. Everyone — to varying degrees — specializes in their own little branch of knowledge. There's no one capable of doing a critical evaluation of the work of someone else who's in a slightly different field.

People don't understand this. Take a simple thing: What are the standards of truth in your particular science? In other words, what does it take to convince you that a dinosaur is green?

What would it take to convince me that there are microbes on Mars? Would I use the same standard as you would? The same standard a preacher from Alabama would use? A factory worker from Detroit, a congressman from California, or a NASA guy whose next budget depends on Congress buying his assessment?

What would it take to prove it? And to whom?

This is a critical question, and one not easily resolved. When I ask my grandchildren how much they love me and they say, "A whole bunch!" well, that's good enough. When I ask my wife how much she loves me, her answer might depend on the checkbook, or on the difference of opinion we had last night about my work schedule. So what are the criteria? It's a very important question.

People also don't understand the difference between experimental science — something that can be repeated for verification — and observational science, which can't. We can repeat the experiment about germinating seedlings, but insofar as the creation of the world is concerned, that's not something that we can replicate. It was a one-time event.

So the best we can say about many arguments, including evolution, is that we simply don't know. We weren't there. It doesn't mean that one side or the other is wrong — it means we don't know. We didn't witness it. No one did. So some people have extrapolated backwards and have voiced their opinions, but the bottom line is, we don't know.

Another simple thing: the age of the earth, the age of time. What evidence do we have?

Well, there's carbon dating. But anyone can tell you that carbon dating is valid for between 5,000 and 10,000 years ago. Anything older than that, it doesn't work. That's not a theological statement. It's just that the science doesn't work for material older than that. Scientists make some assumptions, but that's not fact.

Keep in mind, too, that science changes. What we teach now — compared to what we taught 100 years ago, 200 years ago — is elementally different. I have no problem assuring you that what mankind will be teaching 100 years from now will be different again. A hundred years from now, those scientists will look back at us and smile. We'll be a little arcane, a little dated. We did our best, they'll say, based on what we knew.

I'm not knocking science or scientists. My point is simply that an honest scientist will tell you what he knows and what he doesn't know. He won't lecture out of his field. There's an abundance of ignorance out there, among educated people and brilliant ones as well. We just have to know where it is.

Superimposed on all that is an abysmal ignorance of Torah. Let's take just the first words of the book in question, and see how far we get.

"In the beginning, God created the heaven and the earth ..." Is there anyone who takes exception to that? Easy question: I do.

Most knowledgeable commentators do, and all of them who understand Hebrew grammar know that's not correct. Those words in Hebrew can't mean that — and they don't. They never did. The basic problem is, God did not create heaven and earth "in the beginning." He created light. So what that verse actually says is: "In the beginning of God's creating of the heavens and the earth, when the earth was bewilderment and void, with darkness over the surface of the deep, and the breath of God was hovering upon the surface of the waters, God said, 'Let there be light,' and there was light."

I don't mean to set off a theological discussion. But if the very first words of the Torah are misinterpreted — especially when you get away from the Hebrew — then you have a problem.

In fact, let me interject: If you think that the scientists who are opposed to creation theory, who don't want the biblical narrative taught as an alternative to science, you should know that there are some pretty major Jewish commentators who might agree. They'd suggest that the Torah is not a science textbook, and that if your claim is that you want to learn how the world was created, then you'll trip over yourself, because the sequences offered in the Torah itself are problematical. The great Rashi himself says: "God need not have begun the Torah but from 'This month shall be for you (the beginning of months) because it is the first commandment which Israel was commanded."

So why start with the creation story?

Rashi says because in the future people will say to the Jewish people, you are thieves and scoundrels, because you have stolen land on which previous people lived. So this is here, so that the world should know that God created the world, that it belongs to Him, and that, therefore, He can do with it as He wishes. He can allocate it as He desires. If He has given this part of the earth to the Jewish people, then that's it. He created it. It's His to allocate.

That's the whole purpose of the narrative of creation. It wasn't designed to teach anyone how it was created, but rather that it *was* created. To teach us that there was a Creator, and that it is His decision who lives where.

So much for the basic creationist history. But then we go ahead with people who learn Torah from Gershwin — "It Ain't Necessarily So." Or from Cecil B. DeMille, or Charlton Heston, or even from Michelangelo, not to mention Spielberg, Disney, and CNN.

So the first question is, how much science do you know? What would it take to convince you of the validity of the scientific statement?

Second, how much Torah do you know? Or better yet, how much Torah do you know in context with the instructions given by God to mankind?

Let's move on a bit: God said, "Let there be light" — that's fine. You know the litany: "It was evening, it was morning ... evening, morning." Tevye from *Fiddler on the Roof* makes that "sunrise, sunset."

But wait a minute! Morning and evening? But read it again! The sun and the moon were not created until the fourth day. So what passed for "sun" on the first three days? What kind of "sunset" and "sunrise" are we talking about? It must have been a different kind of light. It couldn't have been sunlight as we know it.

So that calls into question our whole understanding of "days." What does that word mean?

Well, study the Torah, and the answers are there, but of course you won't find any actual description. That, you'll only find in the Talmud. You can't really take the literal words of Torah and think you understand. You need the written commentary to do that.

Three times in the Torah it says, "You shall not seethe a kid in its mother's milk," and it says, "You shall not make a graven image."

Well, here I am. I've never in my life made a graven image. So therefore I must be absolutely free of idolatry, right? Is that what that means? And since I've never even had any inclination to seethe a kid in its mother's milk, I guess that makes me perfect on *kashrut*, too. Or is there something more I need to know?

The Christians don't care — they've dismissed all this anyway. But for a comparison between Torah and science, there's a whole system of dietary laws spelled out in the Talmud. So why is this such a sensitive issue? It's because other people — not our most scholarly sages — have adopted our Book as their own. And we're swept up in the worldwide residual of the Renaissance, anti-clericalism, the whole image of the "man of God" as an ignorant priest who leads a mob of peasants even more ignorant than he.

In modern America, the notion is that clergy of all stripes exist to prevent the rest of humanity from having fun, from expressing themselves, from reaching their fullest potential.

That's a shame, because of course the truth is precisely the opposite. For Jews and our Torah, it is our wisest men who asked the questions. Who tried to discover. Who ask, "Is there a God?" The Torah is the realm of the wise, not the ignorant.

When you really look seriously and intimately into the current Torah–science conflict, one of the most amazing revelations you'll have is that of our ignorance. What's surprising is how little we know, and how little we knew, back when we made all those bold pronouncements.

We still don't know the age of the universe. We don't know precisely how it was created. To be honest, we have some speculations, but no one is going to bet their lives on it, or their mortgage, or even their next weekend.

What came before creation? What came after? We don't even know that! With all our knowledge, we can't even predict the weather more than a week ahead of time. What is 20 meters below us? Who has ever seen a tectonic plate? Can you predict an earthquake?

Maybe, for all we know, the world really is located on the back of an elephant that rolls over in the dust once in a while.

With all our knowledge, we don't know what magnetism is, what gravity is, what electricity is. When all is said and done, what we don't know in science vastly exceeds what we do know.

And remarkably, the same thing is true of Torah. Torah is continuously offering new revelations, and all of them point to the same thing: the unity of everything, of all creation. It's the coherence of it all that points to intelligent design, to order.

There is order, to such an extent that if there is no order, we consider it an aberration. We accept the laws of nature; the very fact that we have "laws" of nature implies that there is order, a system. We've improved the world. We've conquered diseases.

We've solved the problem of hunger in the world. When I was in graduate school, there was a famine somewhere in the world every two or three years. Today, when is the last time you heard of famine, when it wasn't manmade? The natural law makes so much sense to us today because it points to unity and coherence. It makes so much more sense.

The funny thing is that it becomes a bigger struggle to believe in random events than it does in a systematic, purposeful creation.

And that's where the conflict between science and Torah is going to be, if there is a conflict. It's not a question of how old the world is — we don't know. It's not about evolution — we don't know.

The real question is: Is there meaning to all this? Is there order? Or it is random?

To my mind, it certainly points to God, to an all-powerful, beneficent, purposeful creator who is interested in what He has created. If we really accept randomness, then when we get sick, do we say, "OK, I'm sick. I've lost it. The dice rolled, that's all she wrote"? No. We want a doctor. We have an inherent belief that there is a cure, something that can be done. That's not scientific — it's pure belief in order, that there is a cure, or that there will be one.

If I needed any further proof, a conversation I had with a friend of mine, an obstetrician in Ottawa, was sufficient.

I've often marveled at the basic miracle of birth. Every one of us, in our mother's womb, was a real aquatic creature before we were born. We were surrounded by water. We didn't breathe, because our oxygen supply came through our lifeline, the placenta, which tied us to our mother's system. In the womb, our lungs were folded up like a fan, not in use, but getting ready. We didn't need any blood circulation to the lungs, because we weren't using them, so in every one of us, there's a hole in the top chambers of the heart, between the right atrium and the left. The blood comes into the baby's heart, and is shunted immediately from the right to the left, bypassing the pulmonary system entirely.

When the child is born, no matter how long the mother labors, "birth" is practically instantaneous. Once the child's head emerges, it must take its first breath; it's now a land creature, not an aquatic one. It can no longer survive in an aquatic world, but must adapt, instantly, to breathing air.

If a child starts to breathe while it's still in the womb, it will drown. And if it emerges into the air before it can breathe, it will suffocate. There's an extremely short time frame in which the transition must occur.

And that's true not just for humans, but for every dog, cat, cow, mouse, rabbit, any creature that has a gestation period. Every creature must go through this tremendous change.

How does it happen? A most amazing chemical miracle takes place, starting during the labor of the mother. Certain chemicals are secreted by her liver and other organs so that these changes will be triggered at exactly the right moment — so the lungs will inflate, the hole in the heart will close, and the blood, instead of bypassing the lungs, will flow through them and provide the oxygen the child needs to survive.

In my lifetime, the president of the United States — the most powerful man of the richest and most affluent country — lost two babies because they were born a tiny bit too early. Their lungs were not sufficiently developed to adapt to oxygen from the air. Jackie

Kennedy lost two babies — and today, that doesn't happen anymore. We've developed sophisticated chemical surfactants that solve the baby's problem immediately.

Is this the benefit of science? Well, yes. But the truth is, what science has discovered is only what happens naturally in 98 out of 100 births.

We say, isn't science amazing! But is it? Nature — call it what you will — designed this system to work perfectly almost all the time. It was only because it failed, now and then, that mankind set out to find out how it worked. Not to change nature, but to do the same thing as nature already did, virtually always.

How brilliant we are? What great science? Nonsense.

Science has discovered only what the Torah says God created. He created the world. He designed humans to be born in this way. He established the order.

Once in a while, after spending trillions of dollars and uncountable man hours of labor, we find out a tiny part about how He did it.

AUTHOR'S BIOGRAPHY

Velvl was the third child born to Samuel (Shloime) and Sarah Greene (nee Hornick). Both of his parents came to Canada as adolescents, emigrants escaping from the czarist scourge of the Ukraine at the turn of the century. As staunch Zionists, Samuel and Sarah were involved socially and politically in their community. Their three children — Ziona (Zed Bellan), born 1917; Geulah (Julie Margolese), born 1919; and Velvl (William), born July 5, 1928 — were raised in a home filled with relatives and friends. The children's first memories included political meetings and out-of-town guests from the then-fledgling Jewish community in Palestine. Velvl's birth occurred while his father was out of town on business, so the task of registering him for a birth certificate fell to his then-11-year-old sister, Ziona. Aspiring to modernize the family's immigrant status, she registered her infant brother as William, an anglicized version of Velvl.

From kindergarten until sixth grade, Velvl attended the I.L. Peretz Folk School, a Jewish day school that catered to the educational needs of the children in the "Yiddishist" community. The school, named for the Yiddish poet and writer, cultivated the Yiddishist mores and philosophy of Zionism and strong Jewish identity. Throughout his education, Velvl was constantly exposed to the classic authors of Yiddish culture — Peretz, Chaim Nachman Bialik, and Sholom Aleichem — as well as the Poalei Zion philosophy of redeeming and building the Land of Israel. His deep-seated knowledge and use of the Yiddish language as a cultural medium was the basis, years later, of his communication and repertoire with the Lubavitcher Rebbe, Rabbi Menachem Mendel Schneerson.

In junior high school, Velvl, still called William, participated in social groups such as school patrol and parade ground drills. His interest in Jewish education continued with evening classes at the Peretz Shul of his primary school days. He joined the Canadian Air Cadets, where he developed a focus and discipline that would accompany him throughout his subsequent career.

While in high school, as news reports began to trickle out from occupied Eastern Europe of the "special treatment" meted out to the Jewish communities, Velvl's awareness of "Jew" took on global parameters. His participation in the Zionist movement continued through membership in the HaBonim movement and his family's continued connection to the Zionist Socialist movement.

As the trickle turned into a steady flow of reports of Jewish persecution and suffering, William learned that Jews were required to don yellow stars; in a show of solidarity, he and his friends pinned yellow stars on their lapels as well. Next, he took the tram to City Hall and had his name officially changed to Velvl, the Yiddish version of William. Since then his name, title, signature — indeed his very essence — has been Velvl William Greene. This is the name that is printed on every one of his degrees and publications.

After graduating from high school, Velvl took his first steps into the world of higher education and research, a trek that continued until his death in 2011. With the arrival of VE day in 1945 and the newsreels exposing to the world the atrocities of the Holocaust, Velvl began his journey. He completed his BSA at the University of Manitoba, where he was introduced to the concept of bacteriology and sanitary sciences. As befitting a man with the political and philosophical ideals Velvl had been raised with, as well as his parents' insistence that the redemption of Palestine was imminent, Velvl's direction in graduate school was guided by the beacon of agricultural development: to have a career that would implement the declaration of the State of Israel, "drain the swamps," and establish the agricultural basis of food production. He wryly poked fun that he was "trained to spoil milk to the point of cheese and raise healthy chickens to the point of chicken soup." Velvl completed his post-graduate work at the University of Minnesota, earning a master's degree in dairy bacteriology.

In 1951, he took a break from scholastic advancement and accepted various teaching positions, including at the University of Saskatchewan and at North Carolina State University. After spending some time traveling for both pleasure and work, he returned to Minnesota and applied himself to earning his PhD. His thesis was titled: "The Influence of Heat-Induced Chemical Changes in Milk on *Lactic Streptocci*" (*vis a vis* spoilage of milk to the point of cheese).

Velvl was punctual and organized, always working from lists and crossing off tasks as they were achieved. At this time, he had but three items on his short list: 1) finish doctorate; 2) purchase a car; 3) get married. In 1955 he was introduced to a young woman named Gail Chesler. In 1956 he bought his first car — a used 1946 Pontiac — for $300. Keeping to his own timetable, during the same year he was granted his PhD and, later the same week, married Gail.

In 1956, the Southwestern Louisiana Institute lost a court battle to maintain segregation and, under court order, was to become one of the first all-white schools in the South to desegregate. More than half of the faculty members threatened to resign, and a desperate cry for teachers went out to the world of academia. Velvl, a young, idealistic, liberal Jew, accepted a teaching position as an assistant professor. Soon after their marriage, Velvl and Gail moved to the deep South; by mid-1957, the couple was comfortably settled in Louisiana and had their first child, Rachel Naomi.

Due to his work on stemming an outbreak of deadly staphylococcus infection that broke out in Lafayette's operating rooms, Velvl was hired away from Louisiana and moved his growing family back to Minnesota by 1958. Their second child, Peninah Miriam, was born in 1960.

The following year, he was hired as a consultant to the NASA space program due to concern about the possible infection of astronauts by potential extra-terrestrial microbes.

Velvl continued his work in sanitation, disinfection, and contagion control for the rest of his life. He subsequently consulted with various companies that pioneered what we today call "standard procedure": Kimberly-Clark, 3M, American Sterilizer Company, and General Mills. He continued to provide consultation as a researcher for various NASA projects: Ranger, Apollo, Orbiter, Surveyor, and Viking. He also continued his work as a lecturer on public health at the University of Minnesota, teaching more than 30,000 students during his career there and ultimately earning the position of professor emeritus of the School of Public Health.

By 1962, his two daughters were enrolled in school at the Bnei Abraham Conservative Congregation, where Gail was a member of the choir. Through their affiliation with the Jewish community in Minneapolis, they met with Rabbi Meier Eisemann, principal of the local Jewish day school, Torah Academy. The girls were started on their own journey in Jewish education, and the family expanded with the birth of David Isser.

At this time, Velvl met Rabbi Moshe Feller, and both of their lives were changed forever. A native of Minneapolis, Rabbi Feller had been sent to his hometown as a representative of the Lubavitcher Rebbe for outreach programming.

Velvl and Gail honed their religious observance step by step, under the guidance of Rabbi Feller and his wife, Mindel (nee Lew). As Velvl's lecture tours on hospital disinfection and microbiology continued, he also began to make lecture appearances at Lubavitch affairs. In 1972, Nechamah Deenah was born and, in 1974, Shmuel Yaakov.

In 1977, Velvl took a sabbatical from the University of Minnesota and accepted a temporary position at the Ben-Gurion University in Beersheva, Israel. From caring for infants in the deep South to resolving an infant diarrhea epidemic among the Bedouin tribes in the southern Israeli desert, Velvl had come full circle. Although he longed to remain in Israel, at the behest of the Lubavitcher Rebbe he returned to Minnesota and continued his work there. The two older daughters moved to Israel, married, and had children, increasing Velvl's longing to move to Israel. In 1984, Velvl and Gail returned to Israel for another sabbatical. At that time, Ben-Gurion University of the Negev was developing its Center for Jewish Medical Ethics, named in honor of Lord Immanuel Jakobovits, the former chief rabbi of England, and Velvl was asked to chair the center.

In 1986, Velvl retired fully from the University of Minnesota and moved to Israel, fulfilling both his lifelong Zionist dream and his desire to be near his growing family. He continued to work at Ben-Gurion University as director of the Center for Jewish Medical Ethics, as well as a consultant in hospital and surgical instrument sanitation. After his retirement from the Ben-Gurion University in 1997, he continued to lecture for the medical school in Beersheva, as well as for Lubavitch, in Israel and abroad.

His thirst for learning was in constant competition with his passion for teaching. This characteristic continued to the very end of his life. Velvl was at a grandson's wedding, then a week later at another grandson's wedding, dancing and celebrating as he was wont to do at family gatherings. After basking in the attention of children, grandchildren, and great-grandchildren, he went back to Beersheva to continue his daily learning schedule. The next morning, Velvl was on his way to Jerusalem to give a lecture, but instead went to the emergency room. He died at age 83.

Articles and interviews describe Velvl as "affable," "outgoing," and "entertaining," with eyes crinkled in a smile. He was that and more. He was also incisive, concise, logical, and passionate in his beliefs. There was no posturing or playacting for the sake of societal niceties. His faith wasn't based on blind acceptance, but rather a thorough investigation and weighing of the statistical and inherent facts. He was ever the epidemiologist and scientist.

The joy and appreciation of gaining something through toil and effort is incomparably *greater than something which comes by without trying.*

— Rabbi Menachem Mendel Schneerson, 1967

RABBI MENACHEM M. SCHNEERSON
Lubavitch
770 Eastern Parkway
Brooklyn 13, N. Y.

HYacinth 3-9250

מנחם מענדל שניאורסאהן
ליובאוויטש

770 איסטערן פּארקוויי
ברוקלין, נ. י.

B.H. 21st of Sivan, 5725
Brooklyn, N.Y.

Dr. Velvel Greene
Minneapolis, Minn.

Sholom uBrocho:

You have undoubtedly received my regards through Rabbi Moshe
Feller, who had also brought me your regards. I trust you had
an enjoyable and inspiring festival of Kabbolas haTorah, and
that the inspiration will be with you throughout the year, to
animate all your daily activities, inasmuch as the Torah totally
encompasses the daily life of the Jew in all its aspects.

I acknowledge with thanks receipt of your letter of May 9th, also
your works on your scientific research. I appreciate your thought-
fulness and trouble in sending me the material. Although the
subject matter is entirely beyond my province, I trust that I
will be able to glean some general ideas from your writings, and
perhaps also some specific ones.

At the risk of not sounding very "scientific" to you, I nevertheless wish to express my hope that you will apply also your
research work to good advantage in the service of G-d, in accord
with the principle, "Know Him in all thy ways." Indeed, the
discoveries in the natural sciences have thrown new light on the
wonders of Creation, and the modern trend has consequently been
towards the recognition of the unity pervading Nature. In fact,
with every advancement in science the underlying unity in the
physical world have become more clearly discernable; so much so,
that science is now searching for the ideal formula which would
comprise all the phenomena of the physical world in one comprehensive equation. With a little further insight it can be seen
that the unity in Nature is the reflection of true monotheism
in its Jewish concept. For, as we Jews conceive of monotheism ,
it is not merely the belief that there is only One G-d, but
that G-d's Unity transcends also the physical world, so that
there is/one reality, namely G-d. However, inasmuch as Creation
included all the souls, etc., there has been created a multiplicity
and diversity in Nature - insofar as the created beings themselves
are concerned, without, however, effecting any change in the
Creator, as explained at length in Chassidus.

/only

You ask me about my reference to the Rambam and where it contained
in substance, though in different terms, the concepts of the conscience and subconscience of modern psychology. I had in mind
a passage in Hilchos Gerushin, end of ch. 2, in the Rambam's
Opus Magnum ("Yad Hachazakah"). The gist of that passage is as
follows: There are certain matters in Jewish Law, the performance
of which requires free volition, not coercion. However, where
the Jewish Law requires specific performance, it is permitted

RABBI MENACHEM M. SCHNEERSON
Lubavitch
770 Eastern Parkway
Brooklyn 13, N. Y.

HYacinth 3-9250

מנחם מענדל שניאורסאהן
ליובאוויטש

770 איסטערן פּאַרקוויי
ברוקלין, נ. י.

-2-

to use coercive measures until the reluctant party declares "I
am willing", and his performance is still valid and considered
voluntary. There seems here an obvious contradiction: If it
is permitted compel performance, why is it necessary that the
person should declare himself "willing." And if compulsory
performance is not valid, what good is it if the person declares
himself "willing" under compulsion?

And here comes the essential point of the Rambam's explanation:

Every Jew, regardless of his status and station, is essentially
willing to do all that he is commanded to do by our Torah. However, sometimes the Yetzer(Hara) prevails over his better judgment

/in and prevents him from doing what he has to/do/accordance with
the Torah. When, therefore, Beth Din compels a Jew to do something, it is not with a view to creating in him a new desire,
but rather to release him from the compulsion which had paralyzed
his desire, thus enabling him to express his true self. Under
these circumstances, when he declares "I am willing," it is an
authentic declaration.

To put the above in contemporary terminology: The conscious
state of a Jew can be affected by external factors to the extent
of inducing states of mind and even behavior which is contrary
to his subconscious, which is the Jew's essential nature. When
the external pressures are removed, it does not constitute a
change or transformation of his essential nature, but, on the
contrary, merely the reassertion of his innate and true character.

To a person of your background it is unnecessary to point out
that nothing in the above can be construed as a confirmation of
other aspects of the Freudian theory to the effect that man's
psyche is primarily governed by libido, the sex drive, etc.
For these ideas are contrary to those of the Torah, whose view
is that the human being is essentially good (as in the Rambam,
above). The only similarity is in the general idea that human
nature is a composite of a substratum and various layers, especially insofar as the Jew is concerned, as above.

I will conclude with the traditional blessing which I have already conveyed to you through Rabbi Moshe Feller - to receive
the Torah with joy and inwardness, as a daily experience throughout the year.

                              With blessing, M. Schneerson